WHAT THE CRITICS SAY:

A very worthwhile addition...
—**WCBS Newsradio**

Arn... y in a conventional hotel.
—**Travelore Report**

Easi... helpful addition to my travel library... about the almost too-quaint-to-belie...
—**San Francisco Chronicle**

One ... em long, happy, and healthy lives in pr...
—**Wichita Kansas Eagle**

This series of pocket-sized paperbacks will guide travelers to hundreds of little known and out of the way inns, lodges, and historic hotels.... a thorough menu.
—**(House Beautiful's) Colonial Homes**

Charming, extremely informative, clear and easy to read; excellent travelling companions. —**Books-Across-The-Sea** *(The English Speaking Union)*

...a fine selection of inviting places to stay... provide excellent guidance....
—**Blair & Ketchum's Country Journal**

Obviously designed for our kind of travel.... [the authors] have our kind of taste.
—**Daily Oklahoman**

The first guidebook was so successful that they have now taken on the whole nation.... Inns are chosen for charm, architectural style, location, furnishings and history. —**Portland Oregonian**

Many quaint and comfy country inns throughout the United States... The authors have a grasp of history and legend. —**Dallas (Tx.) News**

Very fine travel guides. —**Santa Ana (Calif.) Register**

A wonderful source for planning trips. —**Northampton (Mass.) Gazette**

...pocketsize books full of facts.... attractively made and illustrated.
—**New York Times Book Review**

Hundreds of lovely country inns reflecting the charm and hospitality of various areas throughout the U.S. —**Youngstown (Ohio) Vindicator**

Some genius must have measured the average American dashboard, because the Compleat Traveler's Companions fit right between the tissues and bananas on our last trip.... These are good-looking books with good-looking photographs.... very useful.

—**East Hampton (N.Y.) Star**

ALSO AVAILABLE IN THE COMPLEAT TRAVELER SERIES

☐ *Ferguson's* Europe by Eurail: *How to Tour Europe by Train*

☐ *Ferguson's* Britain by BritRail: *How to Tour Britain by Train*

☐ *Fistell's* America by Train: *How to Tour America by Rail*

☐ Bed & Breakfast America: *Great American Guest House Book*

☐ National & State Parks: *Lodges, Cabins, & Resorts*

☐ MacNeice: *National Sites, Monuments, and Battlefields*

☐ **Country Inns** & Historic Hotels of Great Britain

☐ **Country Inns** & Historic Hotels of Canada

☐ **Country Inns** & Historic Hotels of Ireland

☐ **Country** New England **Inns**

☐ **Country Inns** & Historic Hotels of the Middle Atlantic States

☐ **Country Inns** & Historic Hotels of the South

☐ **Country Inns** & Historic Hotels of the Midwest & Rocky Mts.

☐ **Country Inns** & Historic Hotels of California & the Northwest

☐ Guide to Country New England

☐ Guide to California & Pacific N.W.

☐ Guide to Texas and the Southwest

☐ *Scheer's* Guide to Virginia

☐ *Scheer's* Guide to North Carolina

☐ *Scheer's* Guide to Tennessee

☐ *Scheer's* Guide to Florida

If your local bookseller, gift shop, or country inn does not stock a particular title, ask them to order directly from Burt Franklin & Co., Inc., 235 East 44th Street, New York, 10017, U.S.A. Telephone orders are accepted from recognized retailers and credit-card holders. In the U.S.A., call, toll-free, 1-800-223-0766 during regular business hours. (In New York State, call 212-687-5250.)

The South

COUNTRY INNS
Lodges & Historic Hotels

Anthony Hitchcock & Jean Lindgren

BURT FRANKLIN & COMPANY, INC.

Published by
BURT FRANKLIN & COMPANY
235 East Forty-fourth Street
New York, New York 10017

Copyright © 1979, 1980, 1981, 1982, 1983,
1984, 1985, 1986, and 1987 by Burt Franklin & Co., Inc.
All rights reserved

NINTH EDITION

Library of Congress Cataloging in Publication Data

Hitchcock, Anthony
Country inns, lodges, and historic hotels
of the South.
(The Compleat traveler's companion).
Includes index.
1. Hotels, taverns, etc.—Southern States—Directories.
I. Lindgren, Jean, joint author.   II. Title.   III. Series:
Compleat traveler's companion
TX907 .H5396   1987   647'.947'501
ISBN 0-89102-355-0 (pbk.)

Cover Illustration courtesy of
The Battery Carriage House
Charleston, South Carolina

Manufactured in the United States of America

1   3   4   2

Contents

INTRODUCTION — 5

ARKANSAS — 6

Eureka Springs • Helena • Hot Springs • Hot Springs National Park • Mountain View

FLORIDA — 18

Amelia Island • Cedar Key • Clewiston • Key West • Kissimmee • Lake Wales • St. Augustine • Wakulla Springs • Winter Park

GEORGIA — 36

Atlanta • Augusta • Clarkesville • Columbus • Cumberland Island • Dahlonega • Hartwell • Hoschton • Lakemont • Little Saint Simons Island • Macon • Marietta • Mountain City • Sautee • Savannah • Senoia • Statesville • Thomasville

KENTUCKY — 76

Berea • Brandenburg • Harrodsburg

LOUISIANA — 87

Jackson • Natchioches • New Iberia • New Orleans • Saint Francisville • Wilson

MISSISSIPPI — 105

Natchez • Oxford • Port Gibson • Vicksburg

NORTH CAROLINA 118

Asheville • Balsam • Belhaven • Black Mountain • Blowing Rock • Bryson City • Burnsville • Cashiers • Chapel Hill • Chimney Rock • Clemmons • Dillsboro • Edenton • Flat Rock • Franklin • Highlands • Lake Toxaway • Linville • Mathews • New Bern • Oriental • Pinehurst • Raleigh • Saluda • Tryon • Waynesville • Wilmington • Winston-Salem

SOUTH CAROLINA 170

Beaufort • Camden • Charleston • Pawleys Island • Pendleton

TENNESSEE 185

Gatlinburg • Knoxville • Memphis • Pickwick • Red Boiling Springs • Rogersville • Rugby

TEXAS 197

Austin • Bastrop • Bellville • Big Sandy • Castroville • Eagle Lake • Fayetteville • Fredericksburg • Galveston • Granbury • Houston • Jefferson • Llano • Marshall • Navasota • New Braunfels • Rio Grande City • San Marcos • Schulenburg • Weimar

VIRGINIA 230

Abingdon • Aldie • Alexandria • Charlottesville • Chincoteague • Fredericksburg • Hamilton • Hot Springs • Howardsburg • Leesburg • Lexington • Mathews •Middleburg • Monterey • Mount Holly • Nellysford • Orange • Paris • Richmond • Smith Mountain Lake • Sperryville • Stanley • Staunton • Trevilians • Upperville • Vesuvius • Warm Springs • Williamsburg • Woodstock

*INDEX WITH ROOM-RATE AND
 CREDIT-CARD INFORMATION* 277

Introduction

In this new edition, we have quoted the most recent room rates in a combined rate chart and index at the end of the book. Readers should note that the listed rates are *subject to change*. While the quoted rates are for double occupancy in most cases, single travelers as well as larger groups should inquire about special rates. We list daily room rates as based on the American Plan (AP, all three meals included), Modified American Plan (MAP, breakfast and dinner included), Bed and Breakfast (BB, either full or Continental breakfast included), or European Plan (EP, no meals). In many cases a tax and a service charge will be added. Be sure to ask. Children and pets present special problems for many inns. If either is *not* welcome at an inn it is noted in the description. These regulations also often change, and it is imperative that families traveling with either inquire in advance. Though many inns state they are open all year, we find that many close during slow periods. Call first to confirm your room reservations.

The inns described in this book were chosen for their inherent charm, based partially on their architectural style, location, furnishings, and history. We have made every effort to provide information as carefully and accurately as possible, but we remind readers that all listed rates and schedules are subject to change. Further, we have neither solicited nor accepted any fees or gratuities for being included in this book or any of the other books in this series. We have tried to be responsive to reader suggestions arising out of earlier editions of this book. Should readers wish to offer suggestions for future editions, we welcome their correspondence. Please write to us in care of our publishers: Burt Franklin and Company, 235 East Forty-fourth Street, New York, NY 10017.

JEAN LINDGREN
ANTHONY HITCHCOCK

Arkansas

Eureka Springs, Arkansas

CRESCENT COTTAGE INN

211 Spring Street, Eureka Springs, AR 72632. 501-253-6022. *Innkeepers:* Ron and Brenda Bell. Open April through mid-December.

The whole town of Eureka Springs is a festival of Victorian architecture, and Crescent Cottage is no exception. Located in the historic residential section of town, it was built in 1881 by Arkansas' first Governor, Powell Clayton. Today Crescent Cottage, authentically painted in the colorful Victorian tradition, offers good views of the surrounding green mountains and hollows. In the distance, the statue of Christ can be seen in its setting for the Passion Play, performed each year in the neighboring hills. The inn's back yard has a flower garden designed to provide blooms all summer long. The cottage is decorated with Victorian country antiques and period wallpapers. Quilts top antique oak or painted scrolly iron beds. Breakfast is served in the dining room and is a good time to discuss the day's plans with Ron and Brenda, whose knowledge of the area make them ideal consultants. The inn is within walking distance of shops and restaurants.

Accommodations: 5 rooms, 2 with private bath. *Pets, smoking, and children:* Not permitted. *Driving Instructions:* The inn is on Route 62B in downtown Eureka Springs.

DAIRY HOLLOW HOUSE

Dairy Hollow Road, Eureka Springs, Arkansas. Mailing address: Route 4, Box 1, Eureka Springs, AR 72632. 501-253-7444. *Innkeepers:* Crescent Dragonwagon and Ned Shank. Open all year. Dairy Hollow House clings to a mountain slope in a secluded valley just minutes from Eureka Springs. The inn has been renovated to display a gracious style unheard of in the nineteenth century, when it was built as an Ozark dairy farm's farmhouse. As tiny as Dairy Hollow House is, it has grown in stages. Its history began in 1889, when Daniel McIntyre built the first room. A second room was added the next year; and the final one, in 1925. The three-room farmhouse remained in the McIntyre family until the time of the death of its previous owner, when Dairy Hollow was the last small dairy farm operating in Eureka Springs.

For many years Ned Shank, president of the Eureka Springs Preservation Society, and his wife had longed to purchase the aging farmhouse. With the help of singer-songwriter Bill Haymes they did so in 1977 and set out on their ambitious renovation. At first alone and later with the help of a number of Eureka Springs craftsmen, the innkeepers stripped paint and wallpaper, hand-planed wainscoting, installed etched and stained-glass windows, refinished antique furniture, and commissioned hand quilting for the beds.

One enters Dairy Hollow House through a landscaped garden that is brilliant with blooms throughout the warmer months. After crossing a traditional "set a spell" porch, one enters the parlor–breakfast room, with its original wood paneling now gleaming because of its careful restoration by the innkeepers. An ornate wood stove stands on a brick hearth in the parlor, adding its warmth to the building's central heating in the cooler months. The stained-glass window in this room was made by a local craftsman. It is here that the inn's very special breakfasts are served. Crescent, author of several cookbooks, oversees the menus. The innkeepers provide "rave review" dinners for overnight guests, by advance arrangement.

One of the guest rooms, the Rose Room, has a double bed covered with a Dutch-rose handmade quilt, an Eastlake-style "gentleman's bureau" topped with marble, a cherry night table, and antique hand-hooked rugs. The Rose Room's bathroom has a big old clawfooted tub and a large skylight.

An older cottage was recently renovated, providing two luxuriously large suites that offer more of the fanciful craftsmanship, with tilework, antiques, quilts, and fireplaces to create romantic settings. The "twig wall," made up of a dozen varieties of Ozark trees, is a favorite with guests in the Summer Meadow Suite.

Accommodations: 6 rooms and 2 suites with private bath. *Pets:* Not permitted. *Children:* Under 10 not permitted. *Driving Instructions:* Take Route 62 (Spring Street) past Grotto Spring Cave. Turn right at the sign for the inn, and follow the arrows.

10 / ARKANSAS

NEW ORLEANS HOTEL

63 Spring Street, Eureka Springs, AR 72632. 501-253-8630. Open all year except weekdays November to mid-March.

When it was built in 1882, the New Orleans Hotel was called the Wadsworth. Constructed to accommodate some of the crowds pouring into Eureka Springs to enjoy its health spas, the Wadsworth soon changed its name, first to the Alfred Hotel and then to the Springs. It carried the latter name until 1951 when, because of the elaborate wrought-iron work on the second- and third-floor balconies, it was given its current name. During the 1950s and 1960s, the New Orleans underwent "modernization" that included installation of acoustical drop ceilings, wall paneling, and shag carpeting. Today most of the "improvements" have been removed, and the hotel is listed in the National Register of Historic Places.

An indicator of the success of the restoration was the choice of the hotel for a number of interior scenes in *Belle Starr*, a movie made for public television. The movie company was taken with the lobby, staircases, and restored rooms, and it shot several scenes in them. On entering the lobby, it is easy to see why the movie producers chose the New Orleans Hotel. The spacious room has tall, tin-roofed ceilings, a handsome registration desk and old-fashioned cash register, tall paneled four-square columns supporting the ceiling, and wainscoting rising part way up the walls to meet the bold Victorian wallpaper. At the head of the stairs on each of the upper three floors are smaller guest lobbies that have Victorian touches, such as ponderous old high-back mirrored bench chairs, Oriental area rugs, and small tables with potted plants.

Each guest room is different, and although the Victorian feeling predominates, a few earlier pieces may be found. Some rooms still have to be restored, and not all furnishings are antique, but that is the direction in which the hotel is heading.

The hotel's restaurant has no menu; the bill of fare is written on blackboards. Recent luncheon specials included ham steak, sweet potatoes, and salad, and honey-baked chicken, corn-bread dressing, and cole slaw. Breakfast is also served here. At the underground level of the hotel is another restaurant, called "The Quarter." It has its own cocktail lounge.

Accommodations: 24 rooms, 18 with private bath and 6 with connecting bath. *Driving Instructions:* Take Route 16B into town, where it becomes Spring Street. The hotel is there, in the historic district.

Helena, Arkansas

EDWARDIAN INN

317 Biscoe Street, Helena, AR 72342. 501-338-9155. *Innkeeper:* Martha Hiedelberger. Open all year.

The crescendo of interest in bed and breakfast has been a boon to the traveling public and innkeepers, as well as the salvation of many a grand, but formerly neglected, historic home or mansion. The Edwardian is a perfect example. Built by a wealthy cotton broker in 1904, no expense was spared in creating one of the most elaborate homes of its time in Arkansas. Well over $100,000 later, the broker was bankrupt, and the beautiful building fell into disrepair. Slated for demolition, it was rescued by investors and transformed into an inn, recapturing the elegance of the Edwardian era.

The rooms have period antiques set against a backdrop of exquisite woodwork, beveled glass mirrors, crystal chandeliers, and tiled and carved mantles, enhanced by the convenience of modern baths, telephones, king-size beds, television, central air-conditioning, and ceiling fans. The inn has unusual floors—a wood parquet "carpet" that was created in Germany, applied to canvas backing, rolled up, shipped to Helena, and installed in the house. Breakfast is served in the latticed sun room, while guests enjoy relaxing in the sitting room in the upper hall.

Accommodations: 12 rooms with private bath. *Driving Instructions:* The inn is 60 miles south of Memphis on the Mississippi River.

Hot Springs, Arkansas

MEGAN LORIEN HOUSE

426 Spring Street, Hot Springs, Arkansas. Mailing address: P.O. Box 1222, Hot Springs, AR 71901. 501-624-3926. *Innkeeper:* Barbara Marmer-Chevrier. Open February through October.

Hot Springs National Park is famous for its forty-seven natural springs, which, running under the city, attract thousands of visitors each year. Just across the street from Bath House Row and a block from the brick mountainside Promenade that overlooks downtown is the Megan Lorien House, an Edwardian built in 1888 for the Powers family, in whose ownership it remained until 1980.

Bobbe Chevrier has restored the home, opening the bed-and-breakfast inn as a base from which to explore the historic area. Working fireplaces and Victorian antiques decorate high-ceilinged rooms that retain their original carved woodwork and moldings. Guests have use of a private sauna, and nature trails begin just two blocks from the inn. Breakfasts of fresh fruits, juices, and muffins are set out in the large pine-and-brick kitchen, with its bank of ten-foot-high windows that catch the morning sunlight.

Accommodations: 3 rooms with private bath. *Pets and children:* Not permitted. *Driving Instructions:* Take Route 70 into Hot Springs. At the Motor Queen Lodge, turn right onto Spring Street and drive 3/4 mile to the inn.

WILLIAMS HOUSE

420 Quapaw, Hot Springs National Park, AR 71901. 501-624-4275. *Innkeepers:* Mary and Gary Riley. Open all year.

Mary and Gary Riley have put a great deal of time, energy, and enthusiasm into their inn and take very seriously the business of "bed and breakfast," emphasizing just that — good beds (they had them custom-made) and good breakfast (choices vary daily, with eggs Benedict, eggs fricassee, omelets, waffles, grits, and baked toast amandine appearing regularly).

Williams House is an elaborate Victorian structure built in 1890 and now listed in the National Register of Historic Places. It retains many of its original features and is considered unusual in the area because of its brick and brownstone construction. The building has a wraparound porch and even a stone tower.

Oak and walnut pocket-doors, stained-glass and beveled-glass windows set the mood here. The woodwork is impressive, with paneled wainscoting in some rooms. The inn is furnished throughout with turn-of-the-century antiques and has many antique lighting fixtures. A baby grand piano has a welcoming position by the front door in the sunny entrance hall, which is furnished with a camel-backed sofa and Victorian side chairs. The 12-foot-high ceilings accommodate a towering beveled mirror in the parlor. The atmosphere is most relaxing, with plenty of houseplants in nooks and on fanciful carved oaken and walnut antiques.

Each guest room has its own personality and special touches. The Parlor Suite has beautiful walnut woodwork, a brass bed, and, in its private bathroom, a marble shower and antique pedestal sink. The Front Chamber has an unusual imported French marble sink, with flowers painted on it, and a heavy oaken bedstead, lengthened for comfort. One room has a porch, and another overlooks the garden. Several of the antique-filled rooms can be combined to form suites for families or couples traveling together. The carriage house has two more informal guest rooms with country antiques.

Williams House is just four blocks from Bathhouse Row and the convention and visitors' center. Hot Springs, renowned for its mineral baths, was the first United States national park. Although the area surrounding Hot Springs is quite beautiful, the town itself has attracted a number of amusement parks, restaurants, and giant motel-hotel complexes. Williams House allows guests to escape from all that while still having it close at hand. The town is on Lake Hamilton and near Lake Quachita, known for its undeveloped shoreline and picturesque islands.

Accommodations: 6 rooms, 4 with private bath. *Pets:* Not permitted. *Preschool children:* Not permitted. *Driving Instructions:* Take Routes 7, 70, or 270 to Hot Springs.

Mountain View, Arkansas

COMMERCIAL HOTEL

On the Square, Mountain View, Arkansas. Mailing address: P.O. Box 72, Mountain View, AR 72560. 501-269-4383. *Innkeepers:* Todd and Andrea Budy. Open all year.

Mountain View, in the Ozark Mountains, is known for its hill music and hootenannies. Local musicians can be heard often on the Courthouse Square or on the porch of the neighboring Commercial Hotel. Listed in the National Register of Historic Places, this 1915 Craftsmen-style hotel has been preserved by Andrea and Todd Budy, with original iron beds, antique dressers, and old-fashioned bathrooms. The lobby houses a small gift shop and the adjacent Hearthstone Bakery, where guests and the public have breakfast, lunch, and "baked-from-scratch" desserts. The hotel is less than a mile from the Ozark Folk Center.

Accommodations: 8 rooms, 1 with private bath. *Pets and smoking:* Not permitted. *Driving Instructions:* The inn is 1 block north of the intersection of Routes 9, 66, and 14.

THE INN AT MOUNTAIN VIEW

Route 5, Mountain View, Arkansas. Mailing address: P.O. Box 812, Mountain View, AR 72560. 501-269-4200. *Innkeeper:* Harold McLoughlin. Open all year.

Mountain View, the folk capital of the Ozarks, has Saturday-night hootenannies and other folk-music programs throughout the summer. The town and inn sit in the heart of the Ozark Mountains amid hill-country scenery. The inn, built in 1886, is furnished with Victorian antiques and Oriental rugs on dark-stained pine-board floors. The guest suites upstairs are furnished with period pieces. Guests have use of the parlor and the living room, with its old-fashioned stone fireplace, and rockers line the veranda, where guests can catch the evening breezes. Country breakfasts are served in the breakfast room. The Ozark Folk Center is nearby, as is the Grandpa Jones Family Dinner Theater. The surrounding mountains are perfect for hiking and horseback riding.

Accommodations: 9 suites with private bath. *Pets:* Not permitted. *Driving Instructions:* The inn is a two-hour drive north of Little Rock on Route 5.

18 / FLORIDA

Florida

Amelia Island, Florida

THE BAILEY HOUSE
28 South Seventh Street, Box 805, Fernandina Beach, FL 32034. 904-261-5390. *Innkeepers:* Tom and Diane Hay. Open all year.

Amelia Island stretches for 13 miles just south of Cumberland Island, off the northern Atlantic coast of Florida. Fernandina Beach is the largest village on the island and the home of The Bailey House, a Queen Anne-style bed-and-breakfast inn built in 1895. Designed by George Barber of Knoxville, the building has turrets, gables, bay windows, and fish-scale decorative shinglework. The house was built by steamship company agent Effingham Bailey for his bride, and much of its fine detailed woodwork was probably executed by skilled boatbuilders.

Bailey House has six fireplaces including the largest, in the reception hall, which bears the inscription "Hearth Hall–Welcome All." In the dining room and parlor, both open to guests, are a number of antique pieces including an old pump organ that guests enjoy using. All bedrooms have private period baths with claw-footed tubs as well as separate tiled showers, pedestal sinks, and oaken toilets. Two of the larger rooms have fireplaces. The Rose Room is the most elegant and includes a large sitting area in a turret. Guests enjoy the front porch with its old porch swing and wicker rockers. This is the only spot at Bailey House where smoking is permitted. A Continental breakfast is served to guests.

Accommodations: 4 rooms with private bath. *Pets:* Not permitted. *Children:* Under ten not permitted. *Driving Instructions:* From I-95, take Route A1A to Amelia Island. Take a left on Center Street and another left onto Seventh Street.

THE 1735 HOUSE

584 South Fletcher Avenue, Amelia Island, FL 32034. 904-261-5878. *Innkeepers:* David and Susan Caples. Open all year.

In 1735, Governor James Olglethorpe of Georgia, while on an expedition, marveled at the beauty of a barrier island his party had discovered. He later named the island Amelia, in honor of King George II's sister. Although it was constructed in 1928, The 1735 House takes its name from this significant date in the island's history.

The 1735 House is the only country inn in Florida that directly faces the Atlantic Ocean. The Cape Cod–style frame house is painted white with black shutters. Each guest room is set up like a suite, with an antique-furnished bedroom on the building's street side, a captain's bunk-bed area in the center of the room, and a living room facing the surf. A romantic lighthouse is a favorite with guests.

Breakfast, delivered to the guest rooms in wicker baskets, includes breakfast rolls, juice, fresh fruit, and coffee or tea. The inn overlooks a quiet, undisturbed section of Amelia's 13-mile stretch of beach. It is about 2 miles from the harbor area with its shops and restaurants.

Accommodations: 6 suites with private bath. *Pets:* Not permitted. *Driving Instructions:* From I-95, exit at Yulee, Florida. Go east on A1A to Amelia Island until it becomes South Fletcher Ave.

Cedar Key, Florida

ISLAND HOTEL
Main Street, Cedar Key, FL 32625. 904-543-5111. *Innkeeper:* Marcia Rogers. Open all year.

The Island Hotel, built in 1850 and now listed in the National Register of Historic Places, was occupied during the Civil War by soldiers from both the Confederate and Union armies. Cedar Key is a small community on the sandy island known as Way Key, about 150 miles north of Saint Petersburg, the only occupied island of a group of about forty that dot the Gulf of Mexico coastline. Since World War II Cedar Key has enjoyed a gradual revitalization, although it remains a sleepy fishing town, a sort of living museum of Florida coastal life half a century ago.

The Island Hotel is a galleried two-story building whose exterior is built with tabby, a blend of crushed oystershell and limestone used extensively in northern Florida. The inn's lobby summons up memories of Casablanca with its slowly turning ceiling fans, potbelly stove, and two parrots standing proudly on a perch.

The inn's chef prepares shark "Island Hotel" and soft-shell crab with lemon butter. Grouper and redfish come in several guises, and stone crabs and oysters are served in season. Breakfasts are imaginative.

Guest rooms, upstairs off a parlor with murals, are simply furnished with antiques and "early attic." On weekends, the bar downstairs is usually full, as is the veranda, which makes for a very lively crowd—be prepared to join the activities until midnight. The upstairs veranda is furnished with a hammock for two, a swing, and oak rockers.

Accommodations: 10 rooms, 3 with private bath. *Pets:* Permitted for a fee. *Driving Instructions:* Take Route 24 west to Cedar Key. Turn left on Main Street to the inn.

Clewiston, Florida

CLEWISTON INN

U.S. 27 and 108 Royal Palm Avenue, Clewiston, Florida. Mailing address: P.O. Drawer 1297, Clewiston, FL 33440. 813-983-8151.
Innkeeper: Betty Hill, Manager. Open all year.

The Clewiston Inn is a white brick building with large, crescent-topped, full-story windows and a portico supported by four tall, square columns, built fewer than fifty years ago. The public rooms have beamed ceilings, built-in china-display cabinets, tongue-and-groove pine paneling, and fireplaces. The lobby has a handsome, old-fashioned look, with several couches grouped around the fireplace. Outside are manicured lawns dotted with palm and other semitropical trees and shrubs. The guest rooms are decorated with reproduction Spanish Provincial furniture.

The Colonial Dining Room at the Clewiston Inn is set with white linen and serves three meals daily to both guests and the public.

Accommodations: 56 rooms with private bath. *Driving Instructions:* Take Route 27 directly into Clewiston.

Key West, Florida

DUVAL HOUSE

815 Duval Street, Key West, FL 33040. 305-294-1666. *Innkeepers:* Bob Zurbrigen and Ben Connors. Open all year.

Duval House, actually two Victorian houses painted pastel peach with white highlighting on the balconies and trim, was built in the 1880s as housing for cigar workers. The current owners undertook a full restoration of these homes, a cottage, and two other buildings. This is a tropical-style inn, complete with Bahamian paddle fans, white wicker, Victorian antique French doors opening onto balconies, private decks, and tropical trees and rare plants. The inner garden courtyard has a large banyan tree and many coconut, mango, lime, and orange trees, as well as hibiscus and orchids. A large swimming pool occupies the center of the garden. The pool house has a library, a game room, and a lounge where a Continental breakfast is served.

Accommodations: 21 rooms, 18 with private bath. *Pets:* Not permitted. *Children:* Under 15 not permitted. *Driving Instructions:* Take Route 1 from Miami to Old Town Key West. Turn right at the intersection where Route 1 (Truman Avenue) crosses Duval Street. Drive 1 1/2 blocks to the inn.

Kissimmee, Florida

THE BEAUMONT HOUSE, BED AND BREAKFAST

206 South Beaumont Avenue, Kissimmee, FL 32741. 305-846-7916.

Innkeepers: Rudell and Gerald Kopp. Open all year.

Kissimmee is an old-fashioned Florida town on Lake Tohopekaliga. Strolling the quiet palm- and live oak–lined streets, one is just minutes away from the bustle of Florida's main tourist attractions—Epcot, Disney World, Sea World, Circus World, and Reptile World.

Rudell and Gerald Kopp have restored their Victorian home, built in 1905 on a corner lot surrounded by trees. A lone grapefruit tree shares the back yard with the swimming pool, one of the Kopp's few concessions to modern amenities. The centerpiece of the Victorian parlor is an ornate circular staircase that leads to a balcony and the innkeeper's quarters. Cooled by a paddle fan, the parlor has lace curtains, leaded-glass windows, and Victorian wicker furnishings with chintz print cushions. The four guest rooms are also furnished with period antiques set off by ornate flower and stripe wallpapers. Two rooms have private entrances from the veranda, as well as mahogany fireplace mantels. Antique quilts are on Victorian beds, while matching accessories enhance the atmosphere.

The Kopps are avid collectors of Victoriana and country antiques, and most items are for sale. If you take a fancy to that handsome walnut burl bed or Victorian lady's chair, it can be yours. In the morning, breakfast is served in the parlor.

Accommodations: 4 rooms with shared baths. *Pets and smoking:* Not permitted. *Children:* Under 7 not permitted. *Driving Instructions:* From the intersection of Routes 441 and 192, take Route 17/92 south. Bear right on Broadway and take Emmett Street to Beaumont Ave. Turn left on Beaumont and drive two blocks to the inn.

Lake Wales, Florida

CHALET SUZANNE INN AND RESTAURANT

U.S. 27 and 17A, Lake Wales, Florida. Mailing address: P.O. Box AC, Lake Wales, FL 33859-9003. 813-676-6011. *Innkeepers:* Carl and Vita Hinshaw. Open all year; closed Mondays June through November.

Some inns are done in Early American, some in French Provincial, others in late Victorian. Chalet Suzanne is done in dazzling eclectic. This fairy-tale assemblage of buildings is a testimony to one woman's zeal for living. In the 1920s Carl Hinshaw, Sr., and his wife, Bertha, left Chicago for the warmer climes of Florida. Carl, Sr., passed away, leaving Bertha with only their home, a car, and two children in the middle of the Depression, in the middle of Florida. Undeterred, Bertha took stock of her assets and realized that her years of travel and entertaining had given her an eccentric but solid training for running a restaurant. The Hinshaws went up and down the highway announcing "Chalet Suzanne," named after a daughter. After ten days, a family of four from Miami arrived and stayed two weeks, and that was the beginning of a lifelong tradition of innkeeping.

Chalet Suzanne is a grouping of interconnected buildings reminiscent of a "Moorish-Bavarian" town. Towers, turrets, and minarets are the rule, and stone and stucco blend with wood-shingled "witch's-hat" roofs. There are tile tables in the Swiss dining room, and bathrooms with tiled walls, tiled floors, and tiled, custom-made bathtubs.

The air-conditioned rooms have overstuffed furniture, lacquered tables, parquet floors, imported patterned carpeting, rough plastered walls, porcelain lamps, massive four-poster beds, telephones, and hand-painted tiles. Even the gates to the estate came from foreign lands.

Chalet Suzanne's excellence is perhaps clearest in the dining rooms, which reflect the inn's birth as an eating establishment. As such, it garners awards year after year. The restaurant's stained-glass windows, tiled floors and walls, warm wooden ceilings, and place settings all set the atmosphere. The china collection is extensive, and fresh flowers abound here as they do throughout the inn.

Chalet Suzanne's soups are so popular that they are sold in gourmet shops across the country and in Europe. Dinner entrées include chicken Suzanne topped with an amber glaze, lobster Newburg, lump crabmeat in herb butter, king crab Thermidor, curried shrimp, lamb chops, and filet mignon with béarnaise sauce.

Accommodations: 30 rooms with private bath. *Driving Instructions:* Take either U.S. 27 or Route 60 to Lake Wales. The inn is 4½ miles north of town, on U.S. 27 and Route 17A.

St. Augustine, Florida

CASA DE SOLANA

21 Aviles Street, St. Augustine, FL 32084. 904-824-3555. *Innkeepers:* Jim and Faye McMurry. Open all year.

Casa de Solana is a renovated Colonial home built around 1763. The exact date of construction is unknown, but the house is on a 1764 map of St. Augustine. The cocquina structure, with its carriage house and private courtyard, still has its original hand-hewn beams, pegged flooring, and moldings. The house, in the heart of St. Augustine's picturesque historic district, was transformed into a country inn by the McMurrys, who live on the second floor, where guests are invited to join them for wine and cheese in their living room. The rooms in the inn are furnished with the McMurrys' collection of English antiques. Some of the suites are in the attached carriage house; others are in the main house. An attic suite has sloping eaves and a chimney through the middle of the room. The most lavish of the rooms is the Bridal Suite in the carriage house. All suites have color-television sets, as well as decanters of sherry.

A full Southern breakfast is served in the formal dining room, which has a crystal chandelier and a 10-foot mahogany table on a lush Oriental carpet. If guests prefer, they can have breakfast out on the stone patio in the walled garden, with its lush greenery, palm trees, fish pond, and fountain. The inn is just a few blocks from the water, and the McMurrys provide bicycles for touring historic St. Augustine.

Accommodations: 4 suites. *Pets and smoking:* Not permitted. *Driving Instructions:* Take I-95 to the St. Augustine exit. Turn right and drive to King Street. Turn left and, at the historic slave market, turn right (through the Cochina Archway) onto Aviles Street.

THE KENWOOD INN

38 Marine Street, Saint Augustine, FL 32084. 904-824-2116. *Innkeepers:* Dick and Judy Smith. Open all year.

The Kenwood Inn, a fanciful, sprawling Victorian building in the heart of the historic district of the nation's oldest settlement, is half a block from Saint Augustine's waterfront and the Intracoastal

Waterway. A real find anywhere but especially so in Florida.

Balconies, dormers, and gingerbread braces and supports jut out from every angle of the inn. One porch overlooks the swimming pool. An inviting enclosed courtyard contains large pecan, plum, and grapefruit trees, as well as a fish pond and patio.

Each guest room has been decorated with coordinating wall paints, drapery, bedding, and thick terry towels. Each room is unique, one with lots of wicker, another with walnut pieces and marble-topped bureaus, another with scrolly Victorian oak. Three of the largest guest rooms have king-size beds and fireplaces. Several of the inn's bathrooms sport their original deep claw-footed bathtubs, for luxurious soaking.

Breakfast is a time enjoyed by guests and the innkeepers together, around the big dining-room table in the lobby area. A favorite topic discussed is other inns and innkeepers encountered on travels. In a living room beyond the lobby, guests can relax and read; others prefer the inn's Florida room, home to the only television set in the house.

Accommodations: 15 rooms with private bath. *Pets and young children:* Not permitted. *Driving Instructions:* The inn is at the corner of Marine and Bridge streets in Saint Augustine's historic district.

VICTORIAN HOUSE BED & BREAKFAST

11 Cadiz Street, St. Augustine, FL 43084. 904-824-5214. *Innkeeper:* Daisy Morden. Open all year.

Victorian House is a sunny inn whose pastel rooms are highlighted with stenciling on the walls and floors and Daisy Morden's collections of antique textiles and Victoriana. The many decorative touches include wreaths, dried-flower arrangements, and hooked rugs, many of which repeat the stencil and quilt designs. One guest room has a fishnet canopy over a spool bed covered with a blue-and-white star quilt; another has red and green flowers stenciled on the floor, a red, green, and white hooked rug of hearts and flowers, and a dainty iron bed topped with a floral appliqué quilt.

The inn is in the historic district. On the front porch, wicker rockers and greenery entice guests to sit and enjoy the sea breezes. Breakfast is the only meal served.

Accommodations: 7 rooms, 5 with private bath. *Pets:* Not permitted. *Children:* Permitted in the Carriage House only. *Driving Instructions:* The inn is at the corner of Cadiz and Aviles streets.

WESTCOTT HOUSE

146 Avenida Menendez, St. Augustine, FL 32084. 904-824-4301.
Innkeeper: Ruth Erminelli. Open all year.

Dr. John Westcott moved to St. Augustine in 1858 and soon became associated with northern Florida's most celebrated citizen, Henry Flagler. Both Westcott and Flagler gained fame for their pioneering railroad efforts in the state. Dr. Westcott is also credited with the creation of that portion of the Intracoastal Waterway that runs from the St. John's River to Miami. In the 1880's, Westcott built a home overlooking the Matanzas River section of the Intracoastal Waterway. Today his home is painted pale coral with crisp white contrasting trim. Columned porches span the building's front two stories. Within, the guest and public rooms are among the most sumptuous offered in the city. The centerpiece of the parlor is an elaborate cast iron mantelpiece.

Each of the inn's eight guest bedrooms has been decorated in a different manner. Some have painted white iron bedsteads; others have the dark carved walnut beds characteristic of the high-Victorian period; while still others have stately brass beds. Complementing the period beds is an assortment of antique and reproduction furniture. All guest rooms have plus carpeting and private baths. Amenities at Westcott House are the rule, be it the complimentary wine offered or the sniffer of brandy left at one's bedside. Color television hidden in carved cabinets and room telephones are provided. Breakfast is delivered to guests' rooms on silver trays, or, if preferred, to the white iron tables and chairs set out in the brick courtyard behind the inn.

Accommodations: 8 rooms with private bath. *Pets and smoking:* Not permitted. *Driving Instructions:* Take U.S. 1 into St. Augustine and turn east on King Street. Drive to the bayfront and turn right on Avenida Menendez. Drive 2 blocks to the inn on the right.

Wakulla Springs, Florida

WAKULLA SPRINGS LODGE
 1 Spring Drive, Wakulla Springs, FL 32305. 904-640-7011 or 904-224-5950. *Innkeeper:* John Puskar. Open all year.

Wakulla Springs has been attracting visitors for thousands of years, during which the clear, deep-blue spring and its surroundings have captured the interest and awe of most who have seen them. In the early 1930s, Edward Ball, the financial genius of the Alfred Du Pont estate, purchased thousands of acres of this wilderness cypress swamp and spared no expense building the Wakulla Springs Lodge, a handsome Spanish-Moorish–style inn with marble and cypress used extensively throughout in the floors, stairways, tables, and bathrooms.

The beauty of the Wakulla Springs Lodge has never waned, just mellowed. The building has floor-to-ceiling Moorish arched windows across the entire front overlooking the springs and sanctuary. On the ground floor a spacious porch extends the length of the building. Comfortable wicker furniture and cool drinks await guests who relax here.

Behind the enclosed sun porch is the lobby-lounge. A large stone fireplace has plush chairs and couches grouped about it. The room is decorated with marble floors and has a beautiful ceiling, intricately painted by a German immigrant once commissioned by Kaiser Wilhelm. Every ceiling beam and cross-piece is covered with detailed pictures of the history of Wakulla Springs, its wildlife, Indians, and Spanish influences. Oriental rugs are scattered about groupings of Florida rattan furniture. Marble game tables complete the setting. A glass case in the lobby contains the remains of "Old Joe," the springs' legendary alligator, who was shot in the 1960s. "Old Joe," more than 11 feet long and weighing 650 pounds at his death, lived on a sandbar near the spring and in his day was the most photographed alligator in existence; his death made national news, and a $5,000 reward was offered for information leading to his killer.

Marble stairways and an elevator lead to the guest rooms. Some overlook the springs; others, the wild sanctuary; and still others, the profusion of flower gardens at the entrance to the springs. The furnishings are comfortable, quality pieces from the late 1940s and the 1950s, and each room has its own marble bath. Downstairs, the dining room, reminiscent of a European hotel with rocking-chair seating and white-linen service, offers Southern cooking at its best, including pan-fried chicken, mullets, and country ham accompanied by plates of fresh vegetables—black-eyed peas, baby limas, and navy beans. A favorite dish is the chef's special navy bean soup, on the menu every day by popular demand. There are Apalachicola oysters in season. There is no bar here, and liquor is not available.

Accommodations: 27 rooms with private bath. *Pets*: Not permitted. *Driving Instructions:* The Wakulla Springs Lodge is off Route 61, 11 miles south of Tallahassee.

Winter Park, Florida

PARK PLAZA HOTEL

307 Park Avenue South, Winter Park, FL 32789. 305-647-1072.
Innkeeper: Sandra Spang. Open all year.

Winter Park is a stylish town lined with boutiques and specialty shops and home to several museums, including the Morse Gallery, with its thousands of pieces of Louis Tiffany's work. In the center of town, alongside a shady park, is the Park Plaza. At street level there is little to attract attention to the hotel other than iron gates and flanking boutiques, one a fancy chocolate shop, the other for gifts and flowers. However, the second story veranda is quite eyecatching with its bower of hanging plants and potted flowers designed to screen guests from the street. The lobby has a distinct 1920s ambience: Potted ferns and palms, polished dark woods, marble floors, and an open staircase lit by a roof-top skylight. The small private elevator glows with polished brass, and a big silver bowl of shiny red apples is set out on the reception desk. A sitting alcove has lace drapes on windows overlooking an enclosed courtyard of the restaurant next door. Brocade chairs flank an antique writing desk.

The guest rooms upstairs are small, yet appealing, each with a brass bed, floral-print wallpaper, and its own sitting room furnished with antique wicker and calico prints, as well as paddle fans, television, and telephone. Many of these rooms open onto the veranda.

Accommodations: 27 rooms with private bath. *Pets and children:* Not permitted. *Driving Instructions:* Take I-4 to the Fairbanks Avenue exit. Drive east to Park Avenue and turn left.

36 / GEORGIA

Georgia

Atlanta, Georgia

BEVERLY HILLS INN

65 Sheridan Drive, N.E., Atlanta, GA 30305. 404-233-8520. *Innkeepers:* Bonnie and Lyle Kleinhans. Open all year.

In the quiet residential neighborhood of Buckhead stands the sedate little Beverly Hills Inn, built in 1929 in a symmetrical style chosen to resemble Hollywood architecture of the late 1920s. A parlor complete with a baby-grand piano and a well-stocked library occupy the inn's ground floor and are popular spots for guests to relax in or seek the innkeeper's assistance in planning the day's adventures or the best spot for an evening meal. Many restaurants within walking distance offer a variety of ethnic cuisines.

The inn is furnished throughout with many antiques and period pieces from the 1920s. Oriental rugs cover the natural hardwood floors. Most guest rooms open onto balconies through French doors; some of the rooms also have kitchens. An appealing Garden Room off the enclosed garden is the setting for Continental breakfasts.

Atlanta is a city of shopping areas, museums, music, theater, and other visitor attractions. The inn is convenient to much of this, its neighborhood featuring nearly thirty art galleries, as well as the large Lenox Square/Phipps Plaza with such stores as Neiman-Marcus and Tiffany's, just five minutes away.

Accommodations: 17 rooms with private bath. *Pets:* Not permitted. *Driving Instructions:* In Atlanta, take Peachtree Road north to Sheridan Drive.

Atlanta, Georgia

SHELLMONT BED AND BREAKFAST LODGE

821 Piedmont Avenue, N.E., Atlanta, GA 30308. 404-872-9290.

Innkeepers: Debbie and Edward McCord. Open all year.

Shellmont was built in 1891 by the architect W.T. Downing and is now listed in the National Register of Historic Places. When the McCords purchased the house in 1982, they were only its second owners. A distinctive feature is elaborate carvings both on the building's exterior and within. One dominant theme is shell carvings, augmented by ribbons and flowers. Stained, beveled, and leaded glass abound, and the reception area is adorned with elaborate stenciling. Both the main house and its carriage house are furnished in period antiques and have reproduction wall coverings with a different theme for each of the guest suites. Two in the Main House have fireplaces, and all three have access to a porch. The Carriage House, which accommodates one to four persons, has a living room with a double bed, a separate bedroom, and a fully stocked kitchen. Guests receive a basket of fruit, complimentary beverages, chocolates in the evening, the paper in the morning, and a complimentary Continental breakfast.

Accommodations: 3 rooms and cottage with private bath. *Pets:* Not permitted. *Children:* Under 12 not permitted, except in Carriage House. *Driving Instructions:* From Route 29, drive north on Piedmont to the corner of Sixth Street.

Augusta, Georgia

TELFAIR INN

326 Green Street, Augusta, GA 30901. 404-724-3315. *Innkeeper:* Ms. Pat Hardy. Open all year.

Telfair Street and the Telfair Inn were named for Edward Telfair, Revolutionary War patriot and twice governor of Georgia. The street has a number of significant historic buildings and is part of a restored district called, today, Olde Towne. Olde Towne is within walking distance of the Savannah River and its waterfront area, where many early Augusta businesses prospered. A number of the most successful merchants in the city settled here and built their splendid Victorian homes nearby. The Telfair Inn is a product of the spirit of restoration that inspired the creation of the historic district that surrounds it.

The inn is actually a group of seventeen guest houses. Each is individually decorated and furnished to reflect the period of the buildings' construction, from 1860 to 1890. Some have working fireplaces, and many have whirlpool tubs in their bathrooms. Other modern conveniences include mini-refrigerators, wet bars, and cable television. The suites have kitchenettes. The inn also boasts an outdoor redwood hot-water spa, a swimming pool, and a Jacuzzi.

The inn's restaurant, Fox's Lair Lounge, offers light meals. A complimentary full Southern breakfast is provided for houseguests. The Telfair Inn provides complimentary limousine service to the local airport. Parking is available at the inn.

Accommodations: 92 rooms with private bath. *Driving Instructions:* The inn is in the heart of Augusta's "Olde Towne."

Clarkesville, Georgia

CHARM HOUSE INN

Route 441, Clarkesville, Georgia. Mailing address: P.O. Box 392, Clarkesville, GA 30523. 404-754-9347. *Innkeeper:* Mabel Frye. Open all year.

For those who love the Old South, Charm House is a mansion complete with veranda, columns, wide hallways, and spacious rooms, in a setting on two acres of shaded land next to an 1848 Presbyterian Church. Though formal-looking, Charm House is friendly and casual. Mabel Frye welcomes her guests like long-lost kin, giving their stay a visit-to-Grandma's atmosphere. The inn also has an antique shop.

Rooms are individually furnished with early pieces and "near antiques," four-poster beds, and creaky rockers. All rooms have fireplaces. Breakfasts of rolls, preserves, and beverages are served by the fireside in winter and on the porch in summer. Be sure to hear Mabel's tales of the history of Charm House. (It once served as a maternity ward and hospital.)

Accommodations: 6 rooms with shared bath. *Pets:* Not permitted. *Driving Instructions:* The inn is at the second of three traffic lights on Route 441, in the center of town.

LaPRADE'S RESTAURANT, CABINS, AND MARINA

Route 1, Highway 197N, Clarkesville, GA 30523. 404-947-3312. *Innkeeper:* Robert H. Nichols. Open May through October except Wednesdays; weekends only in April and November.

Mr. LaPrade built his camp in 1916 to house and feed engineers and workers who were harnessing the Tallulah River as a power supply. The result of their labors was Lake Burton, completed in 1925. Mr. LaPrade then had the good sense to turn his camp into a fishing retreat, which has evolved into a rustic Georgia mountain camp just off the Appalachian Trail. Its heart is the dining room, where people come from far and wide to enjoy the truly fresh, home-style Southern dinners. The owners operate three farms providing most of the meat and vegetables served—and the meals are noteworthy. Breakfast features country ham, sausage, red gravy, grits, eggs, hot biscuits, sorghum syrup, honey, and homemade jellies; lunch offers plenty of chicken and dumplings, one other meat, hot biscuits, corn bread, several vegetables, and a cobbler pie; dinners begin with onion relishes and coleslaw, run on through the specialty—fried chicken—or country ham with breads and vegetables, and end with a cobbler dessert. Drinks are included with the bountiful and inexpensive meals, which in turn are included in the room rates for guests.

Guests are reminded that this is essentially a fishing retreat. The food is good, but the cabins are very austere and rustic. Some can sleep up to twelve people each. The cabins are sprinkled around the property; two have fireplaces, and two others are at lakeside. Cabins have front porches with rockers and are outfitted with gas heat and indoor facilities. The camp's Game Room has pinball machines and ice and beverage machines. The marina offers rentals of fishing boats, canoes, pontoons, and motors. The lake and streams offer excellent fishing, boating, and swimming. A gift shop sells mountain crafts.

Accommodations: 21 cabins with private bath. *Pets:* Not permitted. *Driving Instructions:* 18 miles north of Clarkesville on Route 197.

Columbus, Georgia

THE DE LOFFRE HOUSE

812 Broadway, Columbus, GA 31901. 404-324-1144. *Innkeepers:* Jim and Joanne Smith. Open all year.

The De Loffre House is an 1863 town house in the heart of the Columbus Historic District. On a brick-paved parkway, the Italianate house is the epitome of the Victorian period in Columbus.

Public rooms at the De Loffre House include a spacious entry hall that, with several sofas and a table and chairs, acts as an adjunct to the parlor. All rooms, including a second-floor sitting room, are furnished with Victorian and Empire antiques.

The De Loffre House has guest rooms where period lighting, tie-back curtains, and antique beds are the rule. Three of the rooms have a fireplace. Upon arrival, guests find a decanter of sherry and a bowl of fresh fruit in their rooms. A complimentary Continental breakfast is served in the dining room on antique china by candlelight. Several good restaurants are within walking distance.

For those who wish to explore farther afield, the town of Plains, Georgia, is a short drive away, as are Franklin D. Roosevelt's "Little White House," Providence Canyon, and 1850 Westville Village.

Accommodations: 5 rooms with private bath. *Pets:* Not permitted. *Children:* Under twelve not permitted. *Driving Instructions:* Take Route 27 to 8th Street, turn west; go 4 blocks to Broadway. The inn is the 3rd house on the right.

Cumberland Island, Georgia

GREYFIELD INN

Cumberland Island, Georgia. Mailing address: Drawer B, Fernandina Beach, FL 32034. 904-261-6408. *Innkeepers:* The Ferguson Family. Open all year.

Cumberland Island is the southernmost of the Georgia sea islands, saved from commercial development by being made part of the National Seashore. Access to the island is either by National Park Service boat from St. Mary's, Georgia, or by private boat from Fernandina Beach, Florida. The island is a fantasy land of live oaks, southern pines, and — by the sea — marsh grasses and rushes. The area abounds with wildlife including deer, raccoons, wild turkeys, alligators, squirrels, and wild pigs and horses. More than 150 species of birds have been spotted here and recorded by the National Park Service. Overnight accommodations on the island are provided by the Greyfield Inn. It is important to stress, however, that advance reservations are an absolute must and transportation arrangements must be confirmed.

The Greyfield Inn is the last remaining structure of the original Carnegie estate that once encompassed the entire island. The inn's current owners are descendants of Thomas Carnegie's. If you arrive by boat from Fernandina Beach, a Greyfield employee will meet you and drive you down the rough roads to the inn. There is something otherworldly about the drive along the narrow island road canopied by live oaks whose limbs have been shaped to form a tunnel almost blocking out the sun. Guests enter the inn through two rows of brick columns and walk up the broad staircase to the colonnaded front porch that spans the facade. Inside are faint memories of the Carnegie era. Many of the family antiques have been preserved, surrounded by the warmth of dark-stained wood paneling and painted or papered walls. Oriental rugs cover the floors, and turn-of-the-century lamps are the rule. The library's man-high shelves are filled with the classics. The downstairs rooms are softly lit, suggesting an English-style men's social club.

Upstairs are the guest rooms, ranging from some that are fairly small to the two-room "honeymoon suite," which has a sitting room and a bedroom containing a high-backed Victorian bed with an antique white spread.

After a simple breakfast, guests often explore the island on foot, taking along a picnic basket or returning to the inn for luncheon. At dinner, one entrée is prepared each day and dishes include roasts, seafood casseroles, or Southern-style ribs. The inn offers an opportunity for guests to retreat to an island wildlife refuge. The inn's services and accommodations cannot be described as sumptuous, and prospective guests must be warned that transportation on the island is primarily by foot. Those made nervous by wildlife should probably stay on the mainland. The days of luxurious meals served by an attentive staff of servants are far in the past, but the island is filled with eerie romance for those who seek it.

Accommodations: 10 rooms, sharing baths. *Pets:* Not permitted.
Driving Instructions: Advance arrangements must be made for boat service and pickup by the inn.

Dahlonega, Georgia

WORLEY HOMESTEAD BED & BREAKFAST INN

410 W. Main Street, Dahlonega, GA 30533. 404-864-7002. *Innkeepers:* Mick and Mitzi Francis. Open all year; weekends only November to April.

Gold was discovered in the foothills of Georgia's Blue Ridge Mountains in 1828. By 1833 Dahlonega was a full-fledged gold rush town. (The name Dahlonega means precious yellow metal in the Cherokee language.) In 1838 a U.S. Mint was built on Worley land, across from what would one day be the Worley Homestead, an 1845 clapboard building with a classic second-story veranda. The inn was home to Captain William Worley, a distinguished town leader, who lived here until his death in 1913. The homestead later fell into disrepair and was in danger of being torn down when it was rescued by Captain Worley's great-granddaughter, Mitzi Francis, and her husband, Mick. They restored the old homestead, transforming it into a bed-and-breakfast inn, with 7 antique-filled guest rooms, three with fireplaces. Adjoining the inn is a small, two-bedroom cottge, also decorated with antiques. A buffet breakfast is served by staff wearing clothing of Captain Worley's vintage. The inn is set amid many historic buildings surrounding the old courthouse square with its gold museum, shops, and country-style restaurants. Just outside of town are several places where one may still try panning for gold.

Accommodations: 7 with private bath; 1 cottage. *Pets:* Not permitted. *Driving Instructions:* From Atlanta take Route 400 to Dahlonega. The inn is two blocks west of the town square on Routes W52 and 9.

Hartwell, Georgia

HARTWELL INN

504 West Howell Street, Hartwell, GA 30643. 404-376-3967. *Innkeeper:* Mary Jo Swanson. Open all year.

The Hartwell Inn in the rolling hills of northern Georgia is a well-preserved antebellum mansion surrounded by many pecan trees and formal gardens. In true Southern tradition there is a large veranda complete with porch swing and rocking chairs set behind towering white columns. It is one of Hartwell's oldest remaining estates of its kind. Guests enter through a large leaded-glass door into the foyer, which has highly polished hardwood floors and Oriental carpets. They are then given a get-acquainted tour of the public rooms before being shown upstairs to their own rooms. The drawing room, frequently with a fire in the hearth in the fall or winter, is a relaxing room, with reading material, games, and sherry set out for guests. The formal parlor has pre–Civil War furnishings and a grand piano for evening songfests. The high ceilings and leaded-glass windows add to the formal atmosphere. The guest rooms have a variety of antique pieces, including brass, iron, or wooden beds. All rooms have coal-burning fireplaces. Breakfast is served by candlelight in the dining room, which is set up with individual tables decorated in keeping with the season.

Accommodations: 5 rooms, some with private bath. *Pets:* Not permitted. *Driving Instructions:* From I-85 take the Lavonia exit south. The inn is at the intersection of U.S. 29 and Route 77.

Hoschton, Georgia

HILLCREST GROVE

Peachtree Road, Hoschton, GA 30548. 404-654-3425. *Innkeeper:* Dennis Pitters. Open all year.

This turn-of-the-century country house was once the centerpiece of the 2,000-acre Hill-family estate. Although the property now consists of 6 acres, the remainder of the original estate is preserved undeveloped behind the inn. Hillcrest Grove is sheltered by a grove of mature pecan trees in a woodland setting. The Neoclassical mansion took almost four years to complete, and the craftsmanship that went into the building is still evident. The prominent front porch is highlighted by Doric columns and two-story brick pillars, and mahogany is used throughout the interior.

Guests are ushered into a hall dominated by an open-well staircase. The library off this hall often has a fire in its hearth, making it a favorite gathering place for visitors in the cooler seasons. In summer the porch is inviting, with its lounge chairs and frequent refreshing breezes. The guest rooms are furnished with antiques, each has a fireplace, and bowls of fresh fruit are set out on the bureaus. Breakfast, the only meal served, features freshly baked pastries made with pecans from the inn's grove. Hillcrest Grove is an ideal starting point for a scenic drive through the north-Georgia mountains.

Accommodations: 4 rooms with shared bath. *Pets:* Not permitted. *Driving Instructions:* Hillcrest Grove is 48 miles northeast of Atlanta. Exit from I-85 at the Braselton-Hoschton interchange (number 49), then go south on Route 53, two miles to the entrance,

Lakemont, Georgia

Lakemont is part of Rabun County, famous for its setting used in the movie *Deliverance*. The Chattooga River offers excellent whitewater conoeing and kayaking—as the movie illustrated so graphically. Wildwater Ltd. provides equipment and guides. Lake Rabun offers boating, canoeing, fishing, and swimming, with boat rentals and tackle shops. The lake is in the Chattahoochee National Forest wilderness, which has many fine hiking trails and mountain streams with waterfalls and excellent trout fishing. *Tallulah Falls Gorge,* the deepest in the eastern states, once had an enormous waterfall that is now reduced to a small stream. The gorge is off U.S. 441-23 near the Tallulah Falls campground. *Sky Valley Ski Slope* is located in nearby Dillard as is the popular Dillard House, famed for its Georgia food.

LAKE RABUN HOTEL

Lake Rabun Road, Lakemont, Georgia. Mailing address: Route 1, Box 2090, Lakemont, GA 30552. 404-782-4946. *Innkeepers:* Dick and Barbara Gray. Open April through October.

The Lake Rabun Hotel, an old, rustic inn, is across a narrow country road from one of Georgia's most beautiful lakes. In the heart of the Chattahoochee National Forest with its dogwoods, tall shade trees, wildflowers, ferns, and mosses, the hotel is constructed of dark woods and sturdy Georgia stones with planters and stone seats jutting from the stone foundations and chimneys. The inn, built in 1922, retains most of its original work and furnishings and all of its unique charm.

Here many lasting friendships are formed in the informal setting as guests gather around the rock fireplace that warms the lobby. The Lake Rabun Hotel could have come straight out of a fairy tale—couches, chairs, tables, even the picture frames are all handmade of twisty mountain laurel and rhododendron branches. The heart-pine and oak walls display original 1920s art, and the arches have been created out of old pine logs.

The guest rooms are decorated with ruffled tie-back curtains, simple country bedspreads, and colorful quilts that create the feel of a rustic cottage. Two of the rooms still have handmade beds, and most have sinks perked up with ruffled gingham skirts. Guest rooms are cooled by mountain breezes, and the tapwater comes straight from clear, cold mountain springs. No television or telephones jar guests out of this wilderness peace, but the smells of fresh home baking get one up and moving in the morning. Barbara and Dick offer a help-yourself Continental breakfast in the lounge by the fireside on weekends. This is the only meal served, but the neighborhood offers fine "down home" eating at such places as Dillard House and LaPrades Camp.

Accommodations: 16 rooms, 1 with private half bath and the others with shared baths. *Pets:* Not permitted. *Driving Instructions:* Lake Rabun is about 9 miles south of Clayton off U.S. 441-23. Drive 6 miles south of Clayton, then turn right at the Wiley Junction Store and the Clayton Carpet Cleaner. Turn sharp left and proceed 4 miles to the hotel on the right.

Little Saint Simons Island, Georgia

LITTLE SAINT SIMONS ISLAND

Mailing address: P.O. Box 1078, Saint Simons Island, GA 31522. 912-638-7472. *Innkeepers:* Ben and Laura Gibbens. Open mid-February through mid-November.

Every once in a while you are lucky enough to find an inn so private and in such a special setting that you almost feel you shouldn't write about it. One such place is Little Saint Simons Island. Reached only by boat, Little Saint Simons boasts an intriguing history. One of the fabled "Golden Isles" of Georgia, it is said to hide some of Blackbeard's buried treasure. Remnants of thousand-year-old Guale or Creek Indian villages dot the forest floor. Ruins of a tabby (stucco) dwelling built by early European settlers still exist among the thick foliage where wild horses and herds of German fallow deer hide.

The site of one of the first rice plantations on the North American continent, Little Saint Simons was home for a time to the famous English actress Fanny Kemble after her marriage to Pierce Butler. Her book condemning slavery touched off a furor during the years preceding the Civil War and led to her divorce from Butler. Just after the turn of the century, the estate was purchased by Philip Berolzheimer, an owner of the Eagle Pencil Company, which had harvested the largest of the island's red cedars. It has remained as a retreat for the Berolzheimer family ever since. Not long ago the island was opened to the general public on a very limited (twenty guests at a time) basis. Recent visitors have included President Jimmy Carter and Vice-President Walter Mondale.

Accommodations for overnight guests are in four buildings: the Hunting lodge, two new cedar houses, and a honeymoon cottage. Each offers simple, rustic quarters filled with cedar paneling and such quaint country furniture as peeled-log bedsteads. On the walls of most rooms are mounted trophies of the rich hunting and fishing opportunities surrounding the estate. The food at Little Saint Simons reflects its country Southern heritage, offering fresh seafood (fish, crabs, shrimp, oysters, and clams) as well as other traditional dishes like country ham, chops, and fried chicken.

Little Saint Simons itself provides abundant activities for guests with its wealth of natural resources. The island employs two professional naturalists who are expert at steering guests in the right direction for exploration. With 10,000 acres of private land, 8 miles of Atlantic Ocean beachfront, and virtually no development, finding a spot to explore is certainly no problem. Other activities include excellent bird watching, beachcombing, hiking, horseback riding, fishing, or just plain relaxing in seclusion. Along the beach, guests can explore for shore birds, sea turtles, and an abundance of shells. Oysters plucked from the water's edge can become a prelude to a memorable dinner. The possibilities are virtually endless. Stop a moment on one of the island's trails overhung by live oaks draped in Spanish moss and contemporary civilization seems to drift away.

Accommodations: 12 guest rooms with private baths. *Pets:* Not permitted. *Driving Instructions:* The island is reached only by boat. Guests are met at a private landing according to a schedule established when reservations are made. From Brunswick, Georgia, take the causeway to Saint Simons Island. Follow the signs to Sea Island until you get to the intersection of Frederica Road. Turn left (north) and go past Sea Palms Golf Course to Harrington Road, where a large red barn has been converted into a restaurant. Turn right and go to the dock at the end of the road.

Macon, Georgia

1842 INN

353 College Street, Macon, Georgia. Mailing address: P.O. Box 4746, Macon, GA 31208. 912-741-1842. *Innkeeper:* Aileen P. Hatcher. Open all year.

The 1842 Inn is fashioned from two buildings connected by a patio and garden. The main house is a classic antebellum Greek Revival mansion built in 1842, and the smaller is a later Victorian cottage. Together they provide twenty-two guest rooms, sitting rooms, and a formal room for small meetings, luncheons, or catered dinners. All are appointed with Oriental rugs, antiques, and period reproductions. Most of the guest rooms have working fireplaces, and some have whirlpool baths and facilities for the handicapped, along with bouquets of fresh flowers and coordinated drapes, dust ruffles, and bed coverings. Modern conveniences include private baths, room telephones, color television, and central air-conditioning. A Continental breakfast is brought to each guest room along with the morning paper. Other amenities include turn-down service, a cocktail bar in the parlor, and overnight shoeshines. Although the Inn is located close to restaurants, historic sites, and Macon's business district, its landscaped grounds have been planted in keeping with the nineteenth-century atmosphere.

Accommodations: 22 rooms with private bath. *Pets:* Not permitted. *Driving Instructions:* From Macon, take I-16 to the Spring Street exit. Turn right on Riverside Drive and left on College Street. From I-75, take exit 52 and go two blocks toward the historic district.

Marietta, Georgia

VICTORIAN INNS OF MARIETTA-ATLANTA

192 Church Street, Marietta, GA 30060. 404-426-1887. *Innkeepers:* Phil and Kay Secrist. Open all year.

The Victorian Inns of Marietta–Atlanta include the Stanley and Marlow Houses, award-winning Victorian restorations in the historic district of Marietta. Innkeepers, Phil and Kay Secrist, researched the history of each house. Then Kay, as interior designer, and Phil, as historian, furnished the houses with exacting authenticity, with the aid of turn-of-the-century photographs.

Most guest rooms have ceiling fans and ornamental fireplaces, and all—with a bow to modern comforts—have air-conditioning and private baths. The 1887 Marlow House, painted blue with white trim, graces the shaded street with its white fence. The 1895 turreted Stanley House is painted red and enhanced by white gingerbread trim. The parlor of Stanley House has a 1914 player piano for evening sing-alongs, and rooms on its gable floor have skylights over the beds. Both houses have antique-filled guest rooms and suites with sitting rooms. Breakfast is served. On the third Sunday of each month, the inns host a Sunday Serenade that includes a buffet dinner and performances of jazz, cabaret, and classical music.

Accommodations: 14 rooms and suites, 12 with private bath. *Pets:* Not permitted. *Driving Instructions:* From Atlanta take I-75 north to exit 113 (North Marietta Parkway). From the ramp turn left. Follow Clay Street, then turn left onto Church Street.

Mountain City, Georgia

THE YORK HOUSE
    P.O. Box 126, Mountain City, GA 30562. 404-746-2068. *Innkeepers:* Phyllis and Jimmy Smith. Open all year.

The York House is one of northern Georgia's oldest mountain inns. In 1896 "Uncle Bill" and "Little Mama" York opened the inn, beginning a long history of innkeeping for the family. The inn began as a two-story square-logged cabin on a thousand-acre plantation in the Little Tennessee Valley. The walls of the original cabin are now encased within the walls of the living room, den, and two of the guest rooms. The basement still contains a stone room where slaves were once quartered. A stone fireplace in the stone room marks the end of the log cabin, and the original hand-hewn beams and logs are still visible there.

    At the turn of the century, nearby Tallulah Falls rivaled Niagara Falls and attracted many tourists to the region; the railroad increased business when it pushed on through Rabun County. However, when the Georgia Power Company diverted the river's waters to power its hydroelectric generators, Tallulah Falls disappeared. What remains is the oldest natural gorge in North America, more than 2,000 feet deep and a mile and a half long. Today the area is a railroad buff's delight, and many make pilgrimages here in search of remnants, including the old trestles in the nearby mountain passes.

The York House is a tranquil mountain retreat with two stories of shaded verandas overlooking its lawns, towering hemlocks and pines, and the mountains in the distance. The guest rooms, each with its own entrance, are located off these porches and breezeways. The inn's interior is simple and comfortable. Period furniture works to create an atmosphere of timelessness. The rooms have been restored and decorated, turn-of-the-century antiques combining with contemporary comforts such as the modern bathrooms and wall-to-wall carpeting. Full breakfasts served to guests in their rooms are the only meals offered, but there are many restaurants in the vicinity.

The Appalachian Trail can be entered a short distance away. Whitewater rafting and tubing are popular sports on the nearby Chatooga River, and Lakes Rabun and Burton offer swimming and camping as well as scenic waterfalls. Moviegoers may remember that the York House was featured in scenes at the very end of the movie *Deliverance*.

Accommodations: 13 rooms with private bath. *Pets:* Not permitted. *Driving Instructions:* York House is 5 miles north of Clayton on Route 23/441.

Sautee, Georgia

THE STOVALL HOUSE

Route 1, Sautee, Georgia. Mailing address: Box 103A, Sautee, GA 30571. 404-878-3355. *Innkeepers:* Ham and Kathy Schwartz. Open all year.

The earliest section of the Stovall House was built in 1837 by Moses Harshaw, reputed by his neighbors to be "the meanest man that ever lived." His meanness did not hinder his craftsmanship, and he constructed a fine house on a hillside overlooking cow pastures, a creek, and the distant mountains of northeastern Georgia. The following owner, William Stovall, ran the sawmill and made several additions. In 1983 Ham and Kathy Schwartz bought the house and began a careful restoration resulting in an appealing inn listed in the National Register of Historic Places. The wraparound vistas and cow pastures remain, along with twenty-eight of the property's acres.

Stovall House has high ceilings, original walnut woodwork, and a big veranda, complete with old-fashioned wicker and a porch swing. All the rooms are furnished with antiques set off by the polished wood floors and Kathy's decorative stenciling. Each bathroom has Victorian fixtures, including pull-chain toilets, pedestal sinks, and Victorian light fixtures. Ham and Kathy's imaginative Continental cuisine, served to guests and the public, has won accolades from food critics.

Accommodations: 5 rooms with private bath. *Pets:* Not permitted. *Driving Instructions:* Take Route 17 south from its junction with Route 75 (approximately 2 miles south of Helen) for 1 1/2 miles to the junction of Route 255 (at Old Sautee Store); turn left and take Route 255 for 1 1/2 miles to the Stovall House on the right.

Savannah, Georgia

Savannah, one of the South's most elegant and gracious historic cities, sits on a bluff above the Savannah River. General James Oglethorpe and a band of colonists made camp here and laid out America's first planned city in 1733. *Old Savannah* is now a registered national historic landmark, the largest urban area so designated in the country. It is a beautiful city of acre-square floral parks with monuments and fountains, historic homes in a great many architectural styles, ornamental ironwork and moss-covered Savannah-gray bricks, 200-year-old cemeteries, and Southern home cooking. Along the banks of the river is the restoration of Savannah's waterfront, *Riverfront Plaza*, and the charming cobblestone and iron-bridged *Factor Walk*.

There are so many things to see and do here it is almost impossible to list them, much less to give some background. Therefore, the best way to begin a visit to Savannah is to go to *Savannah's Visitors' Center* at 301 West Broad Street, at the end of Route I-16. The center is in the restored Georgia Central Railroad Station, built in 1860. It is open seven days a week from 8:30 to 5:00.

BALLASTONE INN

14 East Oglethorpe Avenue, Savannah, GA 31401. 912-236-1484.
Innkeeper: Paula Palmer. Open all year.

The Ballastone Inn offers travelers Southern hospitality with a generous dash of European elegance. Built in 1835, originally as a private residence, the inn is in the center of the historic district. This area was the first blueprinted in England and laid out by General James Edward Oglethorpe, founder of Savannah. His plans, with parks every few blocks, remain virtually unchanged today, and it is in this lovely parklike setting that one finds the Ballastone.

The inn's name has historic significance to the city. Ballastones were, quite literally, the stones used as ballast in the ships sailing from Europe. When the ships arrived, the ballast would be dumped and the ship's hold filled with bales of cotton for the trip back home. Many of these original ballastones can still be seen on River Street and on the ramps leading up from the riverfront.

The Ballastone is decorated with antiques gleaned from the area's many antique shops, as well as with carefully selected reproductions.

Included in four floors of fine Victorian pieces are elaborate armoires in place of closets, carved mirrors in each bath, romantic ceiling fans, and intimate sitting areas. The beds in each room are reproductions of classic Savannah designs.

At the garden level are smaller rooms, where casual wicker and Victorian oaken furnishings prevail, unlike the more formal upper-floor rooms with their English antiques. Modern amenities include room telephones, television, and elevator service.

Complimentary sherry is served, and there is brandy on the night table. Shoes left by the door are shined overnight. A Continental breakfast, Southern style, awaits guests each morning. In the afternoon, tea and wine are served under the shade of fragrant magnolias and wisteria in the beautifully landscaped courtyard.

Accommodations: 19 rooms with private bath. *Pets:* Permitted with additional charge. *Driving Instructions:* Take I-16 or I-95 into Savannah. The inn is on Oglethorpe Street, between Bull and Drayton streets.

THE BED AND BREAKFAST INN

117 Gordon Street West, Savannah, GA 31401. 912-233-9481. *Innkeeper:* Robert McAlister. Open all year.

The Bed and Breakfast Inn is in two Federal townhouses built in 1853 as part of Gordon Row. The townhouses, once the homes of wealthy cotton planters, overlook Chatham Square, one of Savannah's beautiful parks, originally designed by the city's founder, General James Edward Oglethorpe. The inn is within an easy stroll of the riverfront and the district's museums, restaurants, and major historical sights.

Innkeeper Bob McAlister has carefully renovated the homes, which previous owners had allowed to deteriorate until nothing was left but their shell. Today they are wonderfully restored, with polished wide-pine floors covered here and there with Oriental carpets. Antiques and period reproductions are used throughout the inn. The main parlor serves as an art gallery for Southern artists.

There are two types of guest lodgings here—bed-and-breakfast rooms and garden apartments. The apartments are completely private suites opening onto a garden containing banana trees, flowering plants, and a fountain and fishpond. They have separate entrances, sitting rooms, color television, and kitchens. The bed-and-breakfast rooms, comfortable but simpler, have views of Chatham Square, as well as shared baths. Rooms include a full breakfast of eggs, biscuits, muffins and grits.

Accommodations: 6 rooms sharing 3 baths; 4 suites with private bath. *Pets:* Discouraged. *Driving Instructions:* The inn is on Gordon Street West between Barnard and Whitaker streets, across from Chatham Square.

ELIZA THOMPSON HOUSE

5 West Jones Street, Savannah, Georgia 31401. 912-236-3620; toll-free: 800-348-9378. *Innkeeper:* James Pippen. Open all year.

The Eliza Thompson House is a fine old townhouse built in 1847 for a beautiful redheaded widow and her seven children. "Miss Eliza" and other "ladies of property" used her enormous hearth to bake corn cakes for the Union soldiers in 1864.

Today, the townhouse is an attractive guest house where ceiling fans, courtyard fountains, handsome antique furnishings, fires in the inn's hearths, and the soft luster of the heart pine floors work to create a sense of Southern hospitality in a historic setting. A Continental breakfast is served out in the courtyard, and, in the late afternoon, guests enjoy champagne in the parlor.

Accommodations: 25 rooms with private bath. *Driving Instructions:* The inn is in the historic district, off Bull Street, between Madison and Monterey squares, two parklike areas.

FOLEY HOUSE INN

14 West Hull Street, Savannah, GA 31401. 912-232-6622; toll free: 800-647-3708 (out of state). *Innkeeper:* Muril L. Broy. Open all year.

Foley House Inn overlooks Chippewa Square, with its palms and Spanish moss. The brick-faced inn is composed of two town houses, one built in 1896 and the other in 1870, joined by a stairwell.

The inn is appointed with many antiques, Oriental rugs, pencil-post four-poster beds, and porcelains. Fifteen of the twenty guest rooms have fireplaces, many with elaborately carved mantles. Several guest bathrooms have oversize Jacuzzis, and most are equipped with remote-control television with video-disc players. Breakfast is served on a silver tray with delicate bone china and sterling silver. There are cheesecakes, buttered croissants, and fresh fruits. Guests can take their breakfast, the only meal served at the inn, in their room or out in the sunny courtyard. Guests are offered complimentary cocktails on arrival, turn-down service with chocolates on the pillow, shoe shines, and use of the outdoor Jacuzzi, which accommodates up to eight people.

Accommodations: 20 rooms with private bath. *Pets:* Not permitted. *Driving Instructions:* From Florida or South Carolina take I-95. From Atlanta take Route 75 south to I-16 east. The inn is on Hull Street between Bull and Whitaker streets.

GREYSTONE INN OF SAVANNAH

24 East Jones Street, Savannah, GA 31401. 912-236-2442. *Innkeeper:* James Pippen. Open all year.

Greystone Inn is an 1858 brick townhouse offering guests the best of two worlds: Period furnishings amid the elegance of gracious old Savannah together with the comforts of modern private bathrooms, color television, and air-conditioning. The carefully restored house is decorated with bold floral-patterned wallpapers, echoed by the rich color-coordinated trim. One guest room is painted in deep blues and reddish oranges, with a rich red-orange trim, while another highlights the khaki tans of the background colors of its Oriental carpet and wallpaper with dark-blue floral designs. The rooms are furnished with many eighteenth- and early-nineteenth-century pieces purchased in Charlestown. A second-floor sitting room has French and English wallpapers and period antiques. Two guest suites have kitchens. A Continental breakfast is served to guests. There is a quiet little garden and coveted off-street parking.

Accommodations: 7 rooms with private bath. *Driving Instructions:* The Inn is on East Jones Street, between Bull and Drayton streets.

LIBERTY INN

128 West Liberty Street, Savannah, GA 31401. 912-233-1007. *Innkeepers:* Frank and Janie Harris. Open all year.

When Colonel William Thorne Williams, six-term mayor of Savannah, decided to have a dwelling built for himself in 1834, he chose sturdy materials: local brick overlaid with clapboard. The construction allowed the building to survive several devastating fires that marked Savannah's early years.

The stately, historic townhouse was saved from destruction by Frank and Janie Harris, who bought it in 1967. They have a sentimental attachment to the building. On their very first date, in 1949,

GEORGIA / 67

they went to the Liberty Café, which occupied its ground floor. Eighteen years and five children later, they purchased the neglected property and in 1979, following a thirteen-month restoration, opened their home to guests.

Today, the Liberty Inn offers accommodations in five suites. Each has a private entrance, air conditioning, a telephone, and cable television. The carpeted rooms have handsome appointments such as the original fireplaces, exposed interior brick walls, and original ceiling beams. Iron headboards and period pieces blend with more modern furnishings. Shuttered windows open onto Liberty Street or onto the enclosed garden at the rear of the building, which contains the inn's 8-foot whirlpool spa and a grape arbor.

Each suite has a fully equipped kitchenette whose larder is supplied with Continental breakfast provisions, so guests can enjoy breakfast at their own pace each morning.

Accommodations: 5 suites with private bath for each bedroom. *Pets:* Not permitted. *Driving Instructions:* The inn is on Liberty Street, two blocks east of the I-16 exit.

MAGNOLIA PLACE

503 Whitaker Street, Savannah, GA 31401. 912-236-7674. *Innkeeper:* Ron Strahn. Open all year.

Magnolia Place is one of the grandest of Savannah's guest houses, a magnificent 1878 Victorian overlooking Forsyth Park. Its courtyard and grounds are landscaped with plants commonly used in Victorian times—banana, palms, tea olives and other exotica. A reflecting pool in the garden is home to Japanese carp, while a decidedly unVictorian screened hot tub is tucked into a corner. The house itself is wonderfully High Victorian, with elaborate parquet, marquetry, crown moldings, tiled fireplace surrounds, and delicate woodwork. An open grand staircase is lit by an occulous thirty feet above the parlor floor. The rooms are furnished and decorated with collections of English Georgian antiques, Oriental carpets, porcelains, and brass and silver accessories purchased around the globe. The drapes, upholstery, and bedspreads are all appropriate to the Victorian period. The pencil-post canopied beds are reproductions in king and queen sizes. There are twelve working fireplaces throughout the inn, along with several whirlpool baths, color-television sets, and video cassette recorders, complete with a well-stocked library of cassettes.

The parlor has a melange of antique prints, porcelains, and assorted collections of butterflies, strikers, and brasses. Breakfast at Magnolia Place is served in the bedrooms, in the parlor, on the porch, or in the courtyard, supplemented by complimentary wine at check-in and hand-rolled chocolate truffles and brandy at bedtime.

Accommodations: 13 rooms with private bath. *Pets:* Not permitted. *Driving Instructions:* In Savannah take I-16 to the end and turn right on Liberty Street at the light. Drive to Whitaker Street and turn right. Go past the next traffic light (Gaston Street). The inn is the second house on the right.

17 HUNDRED 90

307 East President Street, Savannah, GA 31401. 912-236-7122. *Innkeepers:* Mr. and Mrs. Richard Lehmkul. Open all year.

The 17 Hundred 90 Inn is in the heart of Savannah's historic district. The beautiful old home is a Savannah Federal; its ground floor is of Savannah-gray bricks, the upper two stories of white clapboarding with shuttered "nine-over-nine" windows. For several years the inn has been a successful restaurant commanding rave reviews. It seemed a natural second step to open the upper floors to guests wishing to savor Savannah's gracious Southern life.

The inn is actually made up of two Federal-style houses joined together. The restaurant on the ground floor has the original gray flagstone floors, brick walls, arches, and fireplaces (there are a total of twenty-six working fireplaces in 17 Hundred 90).

Each of the rooms upstairs is individually decorated for guests; some are starkly modern but most have antiques, wallpapers, fabrics, and furnishings similar to those found in historic Savannah homes. Each room has a working gas-burning fireplace enclosed by glass doors for safety. The fires can be turned on and off by a bedside switch. Two rooms have a large skylight over the bed alcove that is covered with a mirror at the push of a switch. The management pampers guests with bottles of complimentary wines at bedside; breakfasts of coffee, juice, and fresh buttery pastries brought to the rooms in the morning; and hideaway color-television sets.

The 17 Hundred 90 restaurant offers guests and the general public haute cuisine in an eighteenth-century atmosphere. The shuttered room is sparked by plants in the glass-covered atrium. Specialties here are fresh seafood in a variety of sauces, rack of lamb, chateaubriand, shrimp flambéed in sherry, and veal dishes. There is a good selection of wines as well.

Accommodations: 14 rooms with private bath. *Pets:* Not permitted. *Driving Instructions:* The inn is at the corner of Lincoln and President Streets in the heart of the historic district, one block from the Davenport and Owens-Thomas historic houses.

Senoia, Georgia

THE CULPEPPER HOUSE
Morgan at Broad Street, Senoia, Georgia. Mailing address: P.O. Box 462, Senoia, GA 30276. 404-599-8182. *Innkeeper:* Mary A. Brown. Open March through December.

Senoia is a small, old-fashioned Southern town just south of Atlanta. This is *Gone with the Wind* territory, ideal for historical sightseeing and antiquing. The Culpepper House was built in 1871 by a returning Confederate veteran, Dr. John Addy. It served for five generations as the home of one of the area's physicians, Dr. Culpepper. The house's newest owner, Mary Brown felt it would be just right for a bed-and-breakfast inn and set about restoring it in 1982. Interested in historic preservation, she caters to guests who share her love of old houses.

The Culpepper House is an example of Victorian Steamboat Gothic style. The gingerbread trim on the wraparound porch is matched by the trim on the staircase inside. There are curved walls, Victorian oaken fretwork in doorways, stained glass, and pocket doors. Ms. Brown filled the rooms with Victorian antiques, Oriental carpets, and European and Oriental collectibles. She serves breakfast in the old-fashioned kitchen, which has a stone hearth. Senoia and its neighboring towns have interesting restaurants and tearooms, and Ms. Brown will help guests plan outings, including meals and tours.

Accommodations: 4 rooms, 2 with private bath. *Pets:* Not permitted. *Children:* Under 10 not permitted. *Driving Instructions:* Take Route 85 from Atlanta through Fayetteville to Route 16. Turn right and drive to Broad Street. Turn right again and drive to the corner of Morgan Street.

Statesboro, Georgia

STATESBORO INN

106 South Main Street, Statesboro, GA 30458. 912-489-8628. *Innkeepers:* Bonnie and Bill Frondorf. Open all year except Christmas Day.

Statesboro was the center of the Sea Island cotton-producing area at the turn of the century. The inn, a wood-framed country home surrounded by lawns and pecan and magnolia trees, was built in 1904, constructed of local heart pine, with pine wainscotting and ceiling panels. The rooms are furnished with formal Victorian antiques against a backdrop of period floral wallpapers and highly polished floors. The parlor has white curtains gracing tall windows, topped by velvet swags. The guest rooms are fresh and airy, each furnished with Victorian antiques. Modern conveniences such as color television sets, telephones, and modern bathrooms, including two with whirlpool tubs, are incorporated into the decor. Three guest rooms and the parlor have working fireplaces. Full breakfasts are served in the dining room on family china and linens.

Accommodations: 9 rooms with private bath. *Pets:* Not permitted. *Driving Instructions:* From I-95 or I-16, take the Statesboro exit. The inn is in the center of town.

Thomasville, Georgia

SUSINA PLANTATION INN

Meridian Road, Thomasville, Georgia. Mailing address: Route 3, Box 1010, Thomasville, GA 31792. 912-377-9644. *Innkeeper:* Anne-Marie Walker. Open all year.

If you have ever wondered what it would be like living the antebellum life of a Scarlett O'Hara, here is your chance to find out first-hand. Susina Plantation, which opened its doors to the public as an inn in 1980, comes with imposing ionic columns on a classic Southern plantation-house facade. Its Spanish-moss–bedecked oaks, grand halls, spiral staircase, and magnificent chandeliers combine to create "one of the finest plantation houses in the region," according to the description in the National Register of Historic Places—and this is a region that abounds in plantations. The classic square Greek Revival mansion was built in 1841 for James Joseph Blackshear, a wealthy plantation owner with 8,000 acres and 102 slaves.

Inside the house, the work of noted nineteenth-century architect John Wind, one finds a spacious lounge and a dining room with tall windows overlooking the grounds. The rooms have wainscoting, paneled doors, and fireplaces offering welcoming fires on cool evenings. Meals at Susina Plantation are friendly affairs where guests dine together around an antique hand-carved mahogany table under a crystal chandelier. Included in the room rate are a breakfast and dinner with wine, fresh seasonal vegetables and fruits, freshly prepared soup, and a special entrée such as fish au gratin or roast beef. The cakes, pastries, and breads are baked daily in the inn's kitchen.

The inn's guest rooms are furnished with antiques, Oriental rugs, and many Empire-style mahogany pieces. Some of the rooms have antique four-poster beds and hand-crocheted bedcovers. There are large claw-footed tubs in many of the bathrooms.

It is a pleasure to stroll the landscaped grounds with their sweeping lawns, tall shade trees dripping moss, and islands of flowering shrubs and sweet-scented dogwood and magnolias. In all, the inn is surrounded by 115 acres of meadows and woodlands. There is a 3-acre stocked pond as well as a floodlit tennis court and a new 50-foot-long swimming pool. For the incorrigibly lazy, the graceful sweep of verandas awaits, with couches, rockers, and porch swings.

Accommodations: 8 rooms, 7 with private bath. *Pets:* Permitted outside. *Driving Instructions:* Take the Meridian Road (Route 155) from Tallahassee 22 miles north to the inn, or follow signs off Route 319.

76 / KENTUCKY

Kentucky

Berea, Kentucky

BOONE TAVERN HOTEL
  Main Street, Berea, KY 40403. 606-986-9341. *Innkeeper:* Miriam Pride. Open all year.

Boone Tavern is a handsome, white-brick Georgian-style hotel built in 1909 with the aid of student workers. It is operated by a staff composed mostly of students participating in the mandatory student work program at Berea college. Many of the students are hotel-management majors, so that the work experience they gain can be applied in their careers as well as providing financial support. The work program is immediately evident as one enters the inn. Almost all of the furniture in the lobbies and the dining rooms was made by the woodcraft program at the college. Pictures of Abraham Lincoln and Daniel Boone hang on the lobby walls, and the Lincoln lobby has a fireplace, although it has not been used in recent years.

   There are two dining rooms at the tavern. The main dining room seats about two hundred, and there is a somewhat smaller private dining room. The menu at the tavern represents the heights to which Southern "home cooking" can aspire. The kitchen staff has gone out of its way to train prospective chefs and food-service experts, and the results are apparent in the food quality and the cheerful table service. Dinner selections change daily, but a representative sampling might include roast beef, chicken flakes Elsinore with sweet-pepper jam and buttered rice, roast turkey with Southern dressing, roast leg of veal oregano, and our candidate for the dish with the best name: pork chops—some tricky way. All dinners start with one of the tavern's special soups (such as broccoli Roquefort, tomato bouillon, or pureed vegetable) and have relishes, rolls, and Southern spoonbread. Also included are a salad of the day and a choice of two vegetables from a list of six. Desserts also vary each day with such possibilities as Jefferson Davis pie, nut tortes, French coconut pie, or Prince of Wales cake. Fresh flowers decorate the tables.

All guest rooms, which are on the top two floors, have beds, dressers, and chairs made in the woodcraft program at the college.

Accommodations: 57 rooms with private bath. *Driving Instructions:* Take the Berea exit off I-75, then Route 21 north to Berea. The hotel is in the center of the Berea College campus, on Main Street.

Brandenburg, Kentucky

DOE RUN INN

Brandenburg, KY 40108. 502-422-2982/2042. *Innkeepers:* Keith and Kim Hager. Open all year exept Christmas Eve and Christmas.

Doe Run Inn's wooded setting is enchanting, and Daniel Boone's brother, Squire Boone, thought so too. In 1778, Squire and a friend, John McKiney, discovered the stream that runs past the inn. It is a branch of the Ohio River, and they named it Doe Run for the many deer they saw. The oldest part of the inn was begun in 1792, before Kentucky became a state, and the newer part was finished about 1821. It is constructed of heavy, hand-hewn timbers and thick native limestone block. The walls are more than 2 feet thick, and the front door was meant to withstand Indian attacks. Abraham Lincoln's father worked as a stonemason on the building, which began as a woolen mill and has seen service as a gristmill.

The two millstones are embedded in the front walk, the enormous round wooden millstone cover is used as a bench in the lobby, flour sifters are end tables, and the old oak office standing desk still serves. The mill's flour-barrel copper stencils flank the original stone fireplace downstairs. The inn is a stately stone building with a big screened-in porch overlooking the swiftly running stream and the woods. In warm weather, the porch is a favorite spot.

The inn's interior is rustic, with thick beams supporting the ceilings. The limestone walls are exposed and in some places whitewashed. Floors are bare wood in the lobby, and the furnishings are a blend of antiques and family heirlooms. Several of the old kerosine lamps have been converted to electricity. Guests enjoy exploring the inn and discovering the antiques and old prints and advertising art. A tall secretary graces the lobby, and a 100-year-old organ still pumps out tunes. There are old spinning wheels, butter churns, and even yokes used by the oxen carrying flour from the mill.

Of the twelve guest rooms upstairs, those on the third floor are austere but comfortable, resembling nineteenth-century accommodations. The second-floor rooms have more elegant furnishings; the honeymoon suite is decorated with a marble-topped dresser, ornate mirror, and carved walnut bed.

The inn serves three meals a day, every day. The dining room, open to guests and the public, offers Kentucky "down home" cooking. Favorites are the Kentucky country ham with red-eye gravy and the "honest to goodness" Kentucky fried chicken with cream gravy. All meals come with hot homemade biscuits, salads, vegetables, juice, and coffee or tea. The favorite dessert is the inn's special lemon pie. Lunches offer the ham and chicken, and a hearty breakfast might consist of juice, country ham with red-eye gravy, two eggs, baked apples, hot biscuits with butter and jelly, and hot coffee or tea. Smorgasbords, with a groaning board of more than eighty kinds of hot and cold dishes, are served Fridays from 5:30 to 9:00 and Sundays from noon to 9:00. Fridays feature seafood, and Sundays, fried chicken.

Accommodations: 13 rooms, 5 with private bath. *Driving Instructions:* The inn is 4 miles southeast of Brandenburg, Kentucky, on Route 448.

Harrodsburg, Kentucky

Harrodsburg is the oldest permanent English settlement west of the Allegheny Mountains. It was established June 16, 1774, by Colonel James Harrod, who directed the erection of Fort Harrod by Daniel Boone, Benjamin Logan, and John Floyd. At the original fort, George Rogers Clark planned his successful Revolutionary War campaign. The fort has been reconstructed and is now part of *Old Fort Harrod State Park*. On the park grounds are the reconstructed log stockades; the *Mansion Museum*, a brick mansion built in 1830; an early *school building*; *pioneer cabins*; and the *Lincoln Marriage Temple*. All the buildings contain artifacts from pioneer days. The cemetery is the oldest west of the Alleghenies. Every summer from mid-June through August there is a nightly (except Sunday) production of *The Legend of Daniel Boone* in the park amphitheater. The play, by Jan Hartman, chronicles the life of Boone and his contemporaries, including George Rogers Clark, Davy Crockett, Meriwether Lewis, Kit Carson, and Jim Bridger. For ticket information, write P.O. Box 365, Harrodsburg, KY 40330, or call 606-734-3346.

BEAUMONT INN

638 Beaumont Drive, Harrodsburg, KY 40330. 606-734-3381. *Innkeepers:* Bud and Mary Elizabeth Dedman and Chuck and Helen Dedman. Open mid-March to mid-December.

The Beaumont Inn is a fine old Kentucky establishment on one of Harrodsburg's seven gently rolling hills in the heart of the historic blue-grass region. It is a large brick building with a row of tall white columns aross its façade, surrounded by thirty well-groomed acres of partially wooded grounds with rolling lawns and hedges. Here visitors can find almost every kind of native tree and bush Kentucky has to offer; there are persimmons, maples of all shapes and sizes, ash, white pine, and, of course, magnolias.

The Beaumont was built in 1845 as the Greenville Institute, a school for young ladies. In 1855, it became Daughters' College, and after 1894 was known as Beaumont College, until it was purchased by Mrs. Goddard, the grandmother and great-grandmother of the present innkeepers, Bud Dedman and his son Chuck. Mrs. Goddard, who graduated from Daughters' College in 1880 and returned to

teach, eventually became Dean of Beaumont. Her daughter, who attended the school and later took over innkeeping from Mrs. Goddard, has been followed by her son and now her grandson. The Beaumont Inn has received acclaim from newspapers, magazines, and national travel guides. It was recently added to the National Register of Historic Places. The inn and its four generations of friendly innkeepers deserve the warm praise; the place is a well-run, beautifully appointed hostelry, with good Kentucky home cooking.

The inn has been expanded to include two somewhat newer buildings housing additional guest rooms furnished with family antiques and comfortable stuffed chairs for lounging. Some even have the old fireplaces. Tree-shaded grounds can be seen through the white-curtained windows. Two guest suites are in a restored 1921 cottage decorated in early American.

The Beaumont offers fine tennis on newly surfaced (Chevron) courts, swimming in the large pool, which has lights for night use, and many lawn games, such as shuffleboard. The main house contains dining rooms, parlors, meeting rooms, and lounges. The parlors, reminders of the refined old college, have carpeting, rows of crystal tear-drop chandeliers, gilded mirrors above the old mantels, and comfortable wing chairs. During Derby week, parties and private cocktail fêtes are held here.

Hungry diners flock from all over for the Beaumont's famous two-year-old Kentucky-cured country ham or fried chicken, which are offered as the house specialty in tandem. The meal comes with fluffy corn pudding, far more like a soufflé than a pudding, and a wide choice of salads, including tomato aspic, cranberry-orange salad, and fruit salad. The favorite finale is General Robert E. Lee's orange-lemon cake, a house specialty. Several times a week the menu features a dish invented by Bud and his mother called mock scalloped oysters. The secret recipe is never revealed, and Mr. Dedman assured us that no one has ever guessed the ingredients—and it really does taste like scalloped oysters!

Accommodations: 29 rooms with private bath. *Pets:* Not permitted. *Driving Instructions:* From Harrodsburg, go south on U.S. 127. The entrance is on the east side of the highway, ¾ mile from downtown.

SHAKERTOWN AT PLEASANT HILL

3500 Lexington Road, Harrodsburg, KY 40330. 606-734-5411. *Innkeeper:* Ann Voris. Open daily all year except Christmas Eve and Christmas Day.

To understand the Shakers is to understand the beauty-in-simplicity of this restoration, where all accommodations are in the original buildings, furnished as they would have been one hundred and fifty years ago. The Shakers were organized in the late eighteenth century. Part of their religious life involved frenetic shaking and whirling dances, which earned them the derisive title "Shaking Quakers," later shortened to "Shakers," a term they came to use themselves.

The Pleasant Hill village began in 1805, and by 1820 the colony had grown to nearly 500 inhabitants and was prosperous and self-sustaining. The buildings of the village were strikingly handsome, constructed generally of brick or stone under the architectural direction of Micajah Burnett. The graceful twin curving stairways in the Trustees' House are considered his finest artistic achievement.

Today, twenty-seven buildings survive and have been restored at Shakertown. The village now looks much as it did from 1820 to 1850, with a narrow dirt road running the length. The buildings represent the remains of five separate communal living groups called "families."

Visitors to the village may leave their cars in the parking lot and explore the restored village on foot. Although the original road through the village is restricted to pedestrian traffic, a service road runs around the village perimeter, and there is parking behind each of the fourteen restored buildings that have rooms for accommodations. Each guest room has been furnished with authentic reproductions of Shaker furniture. Bedspreads are hand-woven by Kentucky craftsmen, as are curtains and rugs. Some of the rooms are furnished with trundle beds. Each piece of furniture is a copy of an original found in the Center Family House museum. Rooms have concealed air conditioning and all have private baths. In place of closets, rooms have Shaker pegs on all walls.

The Trustees' Office, a three-story brick building built in 1839, is the most elaborate of the structures at Pleasant Hill. There are four dining rooms in the building and several overnight rooms on the two floors above.

Throughout the village, the staff is costumed, as are the waitresses in the dining rooms, which specialize in authentic Kentucky cooking.

Dinner offerings include fried chicken, country ham, fresh fish and steaks, and a daily special. Breakfast and lunch are also served. The management of the dining rooms prohibits tipping (as does the entire village).

The Shaker village is open all year, but crafts demonstrations are suspended from December 1 through mid-March. Two craft shops sell Kentucky handicrafts; and nearby, at Shaker Landing Road, a paddle-wheel riverboat offers cruises from May through October.

Accommodations: 72 rooms with private bath. *Driving Instructions:* The inn is on Route 68, 7 miles east of Harrodsburg.

Louisiana

Jackson, Louisiana

MILBANK

102 Bank Street, Jackson, Louisiana. Mailing address: P.O. Box 1000, Jackson, LA 70748. 504-634-5901. *Innkeeper:* Fran Fetzer Stewart. Open all year.

Milbank is a large Greek Revival mansion with twelve 30-foot-high Doric columns supporting the two-story verandas, built between 1825 and 1830 as a private residence. It is also the oldest commercial building in Jackson, having been pressed into service as a barracks for Union troops during the Civil War, later used as a hotel and dance hall, and, eventually, at the turn of the century, home to a newspaper publishing house. It has now been restored and welcomes overnight guests and tours.

The house is formally decorated and furnished with museum-quality antiques. Guest rooms feature Mallard bedroom suites. (This is the largest private collection of Mallard in the area.) Bears Corner, a restaurant, is on the grounds, serving breakfast, lunch, and dinner. The restaurant is casual, featuring such Louisiana seafoods as redfish, crawfish, oysters, and catfish. Gourmet meals can be arranged for houseguests upon request.

Accommodations: 5 rooms, 1 with private bath. *Driving Instructions:* Take Route 10 into Jackson; turn left on the second street after crossing the bridge. Milbank is on the right on Bank Street.

88 / LOUISIANA

Natchitoches, Louisiana

FLEUR DE LIS INN

336 Second Street, Natchitoches, LA 71457. 318-352-6621. *Innkeepers:* Bert and Mary Ann Froeba. Open all year.

Dating from 1714, Natchitoches, the oldest community in the Louisiana Purchase, has taken pride in preserving its many historic homes and cobblestone streets and has re-created Fort St. Jean Baptiste as it existed in 1732. Natchitoches is also the home of Northwestern University, and many college-related activities are available all year. Fleur de Lis, a many-gabled, turn-of-the-century Victorian house with rockers on its porch, is in the town's Historic District and within walking distance of the riverbank. Its large foyer, living room with a color-television, and dining room are all available to guests. Breakfast, served in the latter room at a 12-foot-long cypress table, includes homemade biscuits, eggs, grits, sausage, fruit, juice, and coffee. The inn's five large guest rooms are furnished in the style of the late Victorian period, with brass, Shaker, and testered beds from several periods. Some rooms have sitting areas, and all rooms display the Froebas' collection of period decorative pieces and memorabilia. Fresh fruit and sherry are put out for guests.

Accommodations: 5 rooms with private bath. *Pets:* Not permitted. *Driving Instructions:* From Alexandria, take Route 1 north to Natchitoches. Follow Route 1 across the bridge and turn left on Second Street.

New Iberia, Louisiana

MINTMERE PLANTATION HOUSE

1400 East Main Street, New Iberia, LA 70560. 318-364-6210. *Innkeeper:* Jane Breaux. Owner: Dr. Roy Boucvalt. Open all year except major holidays.

Mintmere Plantation House stands on 3 oak-shaded acres of land stretching down to the historic Bayou Teche, in the heart of "Cajun Country." Mintmere was built in 1857 as a comparatively small plantation with only eight rooms. It is a Greek Revival Louisiana raised cottage, of a style fairly common in the South from the eighteenth century through the Civil War.

Today the house and grounds have been restored by Dr. Boucvalt and are an oasis in an area that has seen extensive development. The house is furnished throughout with Louisiana antiques of the American Empire, early-Louisiana, and Victorian periods. One guest room has heavy Empire furniture from New Orleans and paddle fans, while another has a cherry armoire and a large tester bed. Guests have the use of the parlor and gallery overlooking the bayou and a duck pond. A full Southern breakfast is served in the plantation's formal dining room.

Mintmere shares grounds with the restored Broussard House, an Acadian plantation house built in 1790. Both are open for public tours. A small 1815 West Indies cottage was moved to the grounds and provides additional guest lodgings.

Accommodations: 5 rooms, 4 with private bath. *Pets:* Not permitted. *Driving Instructions:* Take Route 14 to New Iberia. At St. Peter Street turn right; then continue for 1 1/4 miles to Bayard Street and turn left. Drive 1/2 block to the inn.

New Orleans, Louisiana

FRENCH QUARTER MAISONNETTES

1130 Chartres Street, New Orleans, LA 70116. 504-524-9918. *Innkeeper:* Mrs. Junius W. Underwood. Open August 1 through June 30.

The French Quarter Maisonnettes are seven modern guest rooms, each with a private entrance off the brick and flagstone courtyard of an old New Orleans home. The rooms are part of the 1825 townhouse built by attorney Robert Soniat du Fossat, of the wealthy aristocratic family whose prosperous plantation once occupied the land that is now uptown New Orleans. The pale mauve stuccoed home has the classic symmetry of the Creole houses, with a wrought-iron balcony across the second story supported by graceful S-shaped braces. The ground floor has a center iron gateway leading to a wide, arched carriage drive and the flagstone courtyard beyond. Black-shuttered, full-length windows and French doors flank the carriageway and, upstairs, the wide doorway onto the balcony. For more than one hundred and fifty years, two iron horseheads have guarded the gate and will probably do so for another century or two. Inside the iron gates of the house are several wide French doors with arched transoms opening onto the patio and drive. The interior gate mirrors the arch with fanlike spokes in its iron top. The patio is filled with cherry laurels, a large oak, and tropical plants and vines. Comfortable lounge chairs are placed about for guests' convenience. The courtyard's centerpiece is a three-tiered fountain cast in France in the seventeenth century, its base filled with water lilies. In one corner of the courtyard, a tiny iron spiral staircase leads from the balconies to the ground. It was custom-made for a pair of friendly cats that scamper up and down it with ease.

Guests are given their own keys to the gate along with their room keys; all rooms are entered from the patio. The rooms have contemporary furnishings, and all are impeccably clean, well maintained, and comfortable. Each has air conditioning and heat and a private entrance. Mrs. Underwood includes such extra amenities as a morning paper "delivered silently" to guests' doors and her helpful, privately printed brochure with recommendations on restaurants, night spots, snacking places, walking tours, and such area services as taxis and limousine service, as well as special places off the beaten track. Near to all the French Quarter has to offer, the house is next to the 1734 Ursuline convent and across from another historic shrine, the Beauregard House. Early-morning and late-night snacks can be obtained at the old French Market just around the corner.

Accommodations: 7 rooms with private bath. *Pets:* Well-behaved pets permitted. *Children:* under thirteen not permitted. *Driving Instructions:* The French Quarter Maisonnettes are in the heart of the French Quarter, on Chartres Street between Ursuline and Governor Nichols streets.

HOTEL MAISON DE VILLE

727 Toulouse Street, New Orleans, LA 70130. 504-561-5858; toll free: 800-634-1600 (out of state). *Innkeeper:* Bonnie Leigh. Open all year.

The Hotel Maison de Ville is another world, devoted to comfort and service. Its guests are surrounded by furnishings that transport one immediately back to the court of France. Built sometime before 1742, the Maison appears on every existing early map of New Orleans. In the eighteenth century, its owner, A. A. Peychaud, concocted a mixed drink that included a dash of bitters. He stirred his invention with the quill of a cock, giving birth to the designation "cocktail." Tennessee Williams rewrote *A Streetcar Named Desire* on the hotel patio's wrought-iron tables. The original streetcar is on display in the French Market near the waterfront.

Near the brink of ruin not more than a dozen years ago, the Maison de Ville was saved through a heroic restoration by its new owners, Cornelius White and Terence Hall. The hotel—actually a collection of houses, most of which surround a New Orleans brick patio with a tiered central fountain—is bordered by palm trees. In addition to the Maison, there are four rooms in the converted slave quarters that were formerly connected but are now detached by a few steps. There is also a two-story suite that faces the patio; seven restored cottages operated by the Maison are about a block away. In one of these cottages, Audubon worked on most of the Louisiana portion of his "Birds of America" series.

It is possible to select almost any mood within the Maison's complex of buildings. The Audubon cottages offer an almost stark simplicity, with painted brick walls, exposed beam-and-plank ceilings, and slate or brick floors. This look of country elegance is enhanced by the Oriental rugs and carefully chosen antiques. Each cottage has a kitchen kept fully stocked with welcome items like a full array of mixers, butter, marmalade, and snacks, and each has its own private courtyard and faces the pool and cabana area. In the Maison itself, the feeling is a good deal more formal, with richly colored walls, French chairs and sofas, some bearing the original eighteenth-century needlepoint, marble fireplaces, gilt-framed mirrors, portraits of French gentlemen, and swagged drapes and matching quilted bed covers.

A silver tray brings a breakfast of croissants, juice, and coffee. The Bistro is open to the public for lunch and dinner every day but

Sunday. The menu offers an array of Provençal and Mediterranean dishes, along with an extensive wine cellar.

The Maison de Ville is one of the more expensive lodgings in New Orleans. It doesn't take long here to see why.

Accommodations: 21 rooms, 20 with private bath. Rates include breakfast and complimentary beverages such as sherry and port. *Pets:* Permitted in cottages only. *Driving Instructions:* The hotel is in the French Quarter between Bourbon and Royal on Toulouse Street.

LAFITTE GUEST HOUSE

1003 Bourbon Street, New Orleans, LA 70116. 504-581-2678; toll free: 800-331-7971. *Innkeeper:* C. B. Hightower. Open all year.

The Lafitte Guest House is a restored three-story brick French Quarter structure that was built in 1849 by P. G. Geleisses. On one side of the building, climbing vines have interwoven, almost obscuring the wall. On other sides, the brick is stuccoed in the fashion popular in the quarter. Typical New Orleans wrought ironwork decorates the second-and third-floor balconies on the front and side of the French Manor House.

The owners, Dr. and Mrs. Robert Guyton, carefully restored their guest house and decorated it with period antiques, paintings, and other Victoriana of all shapes and sizes. The velvet-draped parlor recalls the opulence of the Victorian age with red velvets, Oriental rugs, and lush plants. The mahogany mantel is not to be missed.

Many of the guest rooms have crystal chandeliers, typically six glass chimneys surrounding the candelabra bulbs. Furnishings include a blend of modern upholstered pieces and antiques mostly from the 1850–1900 period. Many of the rooms have the original black marble mantelpieces on the room fireplaces. All have coordinated swagged drapes and bedspreads in a variety of floral patterns. The bathrooms are tiled, and all rooms have carpeting, central air-conditioning, and heating, as well as telephones. Five of the guest rooms are in the slave quarters opening onto the courtyard. Here the rooms are appealingly simple, with exposed brick walls and comfortable funishings. In the morning, a Continental breakfast of fresh juice, croissants, jam and butter, and coffee or tea is served. The inn offers free parking to guests, an unusual bonus with accommodations in the French Quarter.

Accommodations: 14 rooms with private bath. *Pets:* Not permitted. *Driving Instructions:* The guest house is on Bourbon Street, at the corner of Saint Phillip.

LAMOTHE HOUSE

621 Esplanade Avenue, New Orleans, LA 70116. 504-947-1161; toll free: 800-367-5858. *Innkeeper:* Bill Prentiss. Open all year.
Jean Lamothe knew the good life. As a wealthy sugar planter in the West Indies, he accustomed himself to surrounding his family with only the finest. In the early nineteenth century an insurrection at Santo Domingo forced the family to seek refuge in New Orleans, which was enjoying opulence thanks to a lion's share of the shipping trade and control of the surrounding plantations. Lamothe constructed one of the area's early double townhouses of brick, probably kilned nearby, although some of the French Quarter houses were built of brick brought down the Mississippi on barges.

As was the fashion, Lamothe built his house with a porte cochere, or carriageway, directly through the center of the house, leading to a central courtyard. The house has cypress floorboards and ceiling timbers that were hand-hewn, and many of its original hand-wrought iron fastenings on the doors and windows are in use today. In 1860, the four hand-carved Corinthian columns were added to the double entrance, and the porte cochere became the main hallway, leading to the twin winding stairways to the second-floor reception area and third-floor suites. The courtyard, made private by closing the porte cochere, is paved with flagstones that were originally a ship's ballast. The courtyard is flanked by the twin service wings that now offer accommodations in rooms once occupied by the house servants.

Like the other fine small hotels in the French Quarter, the Lamothe House has high ceilings and formal furniture. A complimentary breakfast is served in the dining room, and afternoon wine is set out in the parlor.

Lamothe House is decorated as befits Mr. Lamothe's original wealth. Special rooms are the Lafayette Suite and the Mallard Suite, named for one of the most respected nineteenth-century cabinetmakers in the city. Each piece in this room is a collector's item, and the decorative plaster cornicing is among the nicest in the city. The Lafayette Suite is equally distinguished with its pair of canopied four-poster beds, ornate armoire, marble-top dressers, and decorative plaster work. All guest rooms are decorated with Victorian antiques and have private baths, air-conditioning, and nightly turn-down service. Lamothe House is one of a handful of French Quarter hotels that have retained the ambience of an era gone by.

Accommodations: 20 rooms with private bath. *Pets:* Not permitted. *Driving Instructions:* The inn is on Esplanade Avenue between Royal and Chartres streets, at the eastern boundary of the French Quarter.

PARK VIEW GUEST HOUSE

7004 St. Charles Avenue, New Orleans, LA 70118. 504-861-7564.
Innkeeper: Zafer B. Zaitoon. Open all year.

Park View Guest House is in a quiet section of New Orleans overlooking Audubon Park. The St. Charles streetcar, the oldest operating streetcar line in the world runs right past the Park View on its way to downtown New Orleans and the night life of the Vieux Carre. The historic hotel, built as such for the World Cotton Exchange Exposition of 1885, is listed in the National Register of Historic Places. The twenty-five-room Victorian inn has three stories of verandas and balconies overlooking the park and its ancient live oaks. The elegant accoutrements are still here: Leaded and stained glass windows, transoms, and doors; crystal chandeliers; and antiques of a scale befitting the hotel's high-ceilinged rooms. Continental breakfasts of hot croissants and assorted jellies—the only meal at the inn—are served in the Audubon Room, but all of New Orlean's restaurants are just a streetcar-ride away.

Accommodations: 25 rooms, 15 with private bath. *Pets:* Not permitted. *Children and smoking:* Not encouraged. *Driving Instructions:* From I-10 take Carrollton exit to St. Charles. The inn is across from Tulane University and at the edge of Audubon Park.

THE SONIAT HOUSE

1133–37 Chartres Street, New Orleans, LA 70116. 504-522-0570.
Innkeeper: Rodney Smith. Open all year.

The Soniat House is actually two historic town houses joined by a carriageway leading to a common courtyard. One of the houses was built in 1830 by Joseph Soniat du Fossat, a wealthy planter who owned the Tchoupitoulas Plantation farther up the Mississippi. His town house is a fine example of the Creole-American style of architecture at the time of the Louisiana Purchase. In the 1860s an elaborate cast-iron balcony of intricate grape-and-leaf clusters was added. The inn underwent a million-dollar restoration in the early 1980s.

All the guest rooms and suites are decorated with antique Oriental carpets, imported wall coverings, and unusual fabrics, which set off the hotel's collection of period antiques. Many of the rooms open onto balconies overlooking the landscaped courtyard, with its bower of wisteria, bougainvillea, sweet olive, jasmine, and banana trees. Complimentary breakfasts of juice, Creole coffee, and Southern biscuits arrive on a silver tray at guests' doors. Among the many amenities at the Soniat House are valet parking, Jacuzzis, telephones in both bedrooms and bathrooms, imported soaps, and thick, fluffy towels. The Soniat House is in the heart of the Vieux Carré, minutes from its historic sights, fine restaurants, jazz clubs, and shops.

Accommodations: 25 rooms and suites, all with private bath. *Pets and children:* Not permitted. *Driving Instructions:* Leave I-10 East on Esplanade Avenue and take Esplanade to Decatur Street. Turn right, and go a few blocks to Ursuline. Turn right again, and go one block to Chartres Street. Turn right once more; the inn will be in the middle of the next block.

Saint Francisville, Louisiana

COTTAGE PLANTATION

U.S. 61, Saint Francisville, Louisiana. Mailing address: Route 5, Box 425, Saint Francisville, LA 70775. 504-635-3674. *Innkeepers:* Mr. & Mrs. Harvey Brown. Open all year except Christmas.

The Cottage Plantation is quite deservedly in the National Register of Historic Places. The property is located in the West Feliciana Parish, part of the "Garden of Louisiana," which contains one of the largest collections of antebellum plantation buildings anywhere. The mansion is actually a museum that graciously takes in overnight guests.

The land was acquired by a Spanish grant in 1795, and when Judge Butler—whose aristocratic family had been called Honor's Band by George Washington in honor of its military exploits—purchased the property in 1811, it was named China Trees after the long rows of Chinese-fern trees along the red clay bluff. The plantation house is at the end of Cottage Lane, a 3/4-mile-long path that winds through the peaceful woodland off the highway. It is surrounded by a parklike setting with moss-draped shade trees and two English gardens containing japonicas and azaleas. The house was built in three sections, the first in 1795 and the last two in 1810 and 1850. The original section is Spanish in style with spacious rooms opening through French doors onto deep porches (or galleries, as they are called in Louisiana). The doorways are topped with delicate fretwork in gracefully arched transoms. The entire cottage is built of hand-hewn cypress, except for the thick 16- by 16-inch sills of poplar. All the woodwork is well crafted, inside and out. Every room has a hand-carved mantel, some with sunbursts and fluted Doric columns. Museum pieces and family heirlooms fill the house and blend with the original wall-coverings and Brussels carpets to add to the antebellum ambience. Here are hand-carved sideboards that display rare glass and china pieces, luxurious furniture of rosewood and mahogany, some with their original brocade upholstery, and large armoires and canopied bedsteads with lacy valances.

Guests at the plantation have the opportunity to sample life as it was lived on a luxurious Southern estate before the Civil War. The guest rooms have antique furnishings and decor as well as television, air conditioning, and central heating. A wake-up pot of coffee is brought to rooms at 8 A.M.; later, a Southern breakfast of eggs, grits, hot biscuits, and bacon is served in the main dining room. This is followed by a tour of the house, grounds, and outbuildings, including the original schoolhouse, slave quarters, milk house, outside kitchen, carriage and horse barns, and Judge Butler's law offices. The plantation has furnishings, diaries, mementos, and correspondence of the influential Butler family, including letters from some of the most prestigious figures in American history. Beyond the cottage and the outbuildings lie pastures, an ancient orchard, and a tiny cemetery. Tours of the Cottage Plantation are open to the public, and the old kitchen now contains a gift-antique shop. There is a swimming pool and restaurant for guests.

Accommodations: 6 rooms with private bath. *Pets:* Not permitted. *Driving Instructions:* The Cottage Plantation is 6 miles north of Saint Francisville off U.S. 61 on Cottage Lane, which is the driveway of the plantation.

Wilson, Louisiana

GLENCOE PLANTATION
Route 68, Wilson, Louisiana. Mailing address: P.O. Box 178, Wilson, LA 70789. 504-629-5387. *Innkeeper:* W. Jerome Westerfield, Jr. Open all year.

Glencoe is in the heart of "plantation country," surrounded by 1,038 acres of rolling hills with landscaped grounds and gardens of azaleas, camellias, myrtles, and magnolias. Century-old live oaks shade the lawns. The original plantation house was built in 1870, but it burned down in 1898. The present turreted, gingerbreaded manor house, erected in 1903 on the same foundation, is considered one of the finest examples of Queen Anne–style Victorian Gothic in Louisiana. The rooms are furnished and decorated in keeping with the turn of the century. Each of the four guest rooms in the main house opens onto a gingerbreaded porch complete with comfortable old rocking chairs. Eight other guest rooms are in Victorian-style cottages of recent vintage. Each of these has king-size beds and Victorian appointments. Guests are welcome to explore the plantation and use the swimming, fishing, and hiking facilities, as well as the lighted tennis court. Breakfast is served to overnight guests, and other meals are available to guests and the public by advance reservation.

Accommodations: 12 rooms with private bath. *Pets:* Not permitted. *Driving Instructions:* Take U.S. 61 north from Baton Rouge. Turn onto Route 68 and drive 15½ miles north.

Mississippi

Natchez, Mississippi

THE BURN

712 North Union Street, Natchez, MS 39120. 601-445-8566 or 442-1344. *Innkeepers:* Mayor and Mrs. Tony Byrne. Open all year.

The antebellum South waits, alive and well, in Natchez, Mississippi. The Burn was built in 1832 by John Walworth, a passenger on a steamboat down the Mississippi to New Orleans. When the boat docked in Natchez, Walworth decided to stroll through the town to have a look around. He never left.

Walworth built his home in classic Greek Revival style. The overhung second floor forms the roof of the front porch, which is supported by four fluted Greek columns. Gardens slope away from the home on all sides, with more than one hundred and twenty-five varieties of camellias and other shrubs and flowers. The herb garden, with the oldest fountain in Natchez, faces the Garçonnièrre, a guest house. The Burn, Scottish for "brook," was named by Walworth after the stream that passed through the property. Ironically, The Burn did suffer a fire shortly after it was built, and the second floor was rebuilt in the style that survives today. During the Civil War, the house was used as headquarters by Federal troops and later became a hospital for Union soldiers.

Today, The Burn contains a priceless collection of eighteenth- and nineteenth-century antiques. It has a semispiral, unsupported stair-

106 / MISSISSIPPI

way in the front entrance hall. On the wall is a gilt-framed mirror, just one of a number of mirrors throughout the house. A fine crystal chandelier, also one of many, hangs at the foot of the stairs. The Burn has a collection of furniture and accessories any museum would be proud of, but these antiques are part of the house and are used. Upstairs is a huge canopy bed that has been attributed to a renowned New Orleans cabinetmaker. There are dozens of Empire and earlier chairs, dressers, armoires, and sofas. Many of the rugs are Aubusson; the draperies were imported from Belgium. Each lighting fixture is a carefully wired original piece.

Overnight guests are given rooms in the main house and Garçonnièrre, where among the furnishings there is an acanthus-carved four-poster canopy bed covered by an antique hand-crocheted spread. Each of the rooms has a private bath, air-conditioner, and television. The downstairs parlor and informal dining room are where the guests gather for fellowship and Southern hospitality. A plantation breakfast is served to all guests, and dinner is available on request.

Accommodations: 6 rooms with private bath. *Children:* Only school-age. *Pets:* Not permitted. *Driving Instructions:* From the center of town, take State, Franklin, High, or Madison streets to Union Street, then take Union to The Burn, which is between B and Oak streets.

LINDEN

Linden Place, Natchez, MS 39120. 601-445-5472. *Innkeeper:* Jeanette S. Feltus. Open all year.

Linden is an outstanding example of antebellum architecture. The imposing portico across the entire length of the mansion, the balustraded upper gallery, and the parklike grounds of oaks and cedars dripping Spanish moss all work a powerful magic that instantly transports visitors back to a more genteel era. The elegant Federal-style mansion, built in three sections between 1790 and 1849, has been the residence of one family for six generations. Jeanette Feltus and her family still live here, opening their home to overnight visitors.

Houseguests are surrounded by the grandeur of a wealthy cotton merchant's eighteenth-century home. Many of the pieces in the home are family heirlooms dating from the eighteenth and nineteenth centuries and brought here from all over the world. Guest rooms are furnished with canopied four-poster beds set on fine Persian carpets. Their walls are decorated with rare prints and oil paintings, and on display are Chinese porcelains and French crystal.

Guests are served a breakfast of homemade biscuits, eggs, and ham and grits and then given a tour of the house. Jeanette Feltus loves Linden and certainly knows its history and even its secrets. Lucky houseguests hear stories of the many escapades of resident ghosts.

Accommodations: 7 rooms with private bath. *Pets:* Not permitted. *Children:* Under ten not permitted. *Driving Instructions:* Linden is in the historic district of Natchez, off Melrose Avenue.

MONMOUTH PLANTATION

Corner of Melrose Avenue and John A. Quitman Parkway, Natchez, Mississippi. Mailing address: P.O. Box 1736, Natchez, MS 39120. 601-442-5852 or 800-828-4531. *Innkeeper:* Bob Kenna. Open all year.

There is no better way to get the feeling of the opulent life-style of an antebellum Mississippi plantation than to stay at a Natchez mansion, and certainly none has been more handsomely restored than the *circa*-1818 former home of John A. Quitman. Quitman, a governor of Mississippi and later a U.S. congressman from Adams County, purchased Monmouth for his bride, Eliza, in 1826. Today the stately, columned mansion is a veritable museum of Civil War memorabilia, as well as many personal items from the Quitman collection, including the gold sword presented to Quitman by President Polk in honorof his brave leadership of troops during the war with Mexico. Listed in the National Register of Historic Places, Monmouth Plantation is open daily to visitors, and overnight guests may tour the mansion without charge. The John Quitman Room, where guests may stay, has an over-

size four-poster, a velvet-swagged tester, Oriental carpeting, oil paintings, and a decorative but nonworking fireplace. It should be noted that this room is part of the house tour; so guests who wish to use their room during the day will probably be happier in any of the other guest rooms. These rooms all have canopied beds, antique armoires, air conditioning, private telephones, cable television, and wall-to-wall carpeting. The mansion has four guest rooms and one suite. Four more guest rooms are in what were originally the slave quarters, a brick building that could stand alone as a country inn. Other guest rooms are located in two restored cottages on the estate. A full breakfast is served to overnight guests in the original slave kitchen, which is furnished as it was in 1840, and cocktails and hors d'oeuvres are served in the late afternoon. Surrounding the mansion are 26 acres of grounds, which guests are free to explore.

Accommodations: 14 rooms with private bath; 1 suite. *Pets:* Not permitted. *Children:* Under 14 not permitted. *Driving Instructions:* The plantation is a mile east of the center of Natchez.

SILVER STREET INN

1 Silver Street, Natchez, Mississippi. Mailing address: P.O. Box 1224, Natchez, MS 39120. 601-442-4221. *Innkeeper:* Lu Barraza. Open all year.

The Silver Street Inn is an 1840s wood-framed building on a cliff overlooking the mighty Mississippi River. A fairly colorful imagination is needed to conjure up this tidy, quaint little inn's past. Everything is so pristine and proper these days, with rag rugs on polished bare-wood floors, painted iron beds color-coordinated with the floral-print wallpapers and quilts. But in the wild and woolly days of riverboat gamblers just off the paddle wheelers, the inn was a well-known house of ill repute. Today all that is left of its bawdy past is a collection of tales and "Madame," an almost life-size doll who greets visitors in the hall.

The Silver Street Inn has been restored and decorated under the watchful eyes of her innkeepers, who also run the dress shop on the ground floor. The inn itself occupies the second story of the building. Several rooms overlook the river where Mississippi paddle wheelers still dock on cruises out of New Orleans. The upper veranda is lined with rockers, and guests frequently gather there to watch the evening sun go down over the river. The living room is a popular spot, with its working fireplaces and attractive Mississippi antique pieces. No meals are served.

Accommodations: 4 rooms, 2 with private bath. *Driving Instructions:* The inn is on Silver Street in Natchez-under-the-Hill, alongside the Mississippi River.

Oxford, Mississippi

THE OLIVER-BRITT HOUSE INN AND TEA ROOM

512 Van Buren Avenue, Oxford, MS 38655. 601-234-8043. *Innkeepers:* Mrs. Mary Ann Britt and Mrs. Glynn Oliver. Open all year.

Oxford and its environs were the inspiration for William Faulkner, whose mythical Yoknapatawpa County sprang from his lifetime knowledge of the region. Faulkner's Oxford home, Rowan Oak, attracts scholars and visitors from around the world. Oxford is also home to the University of Mississippi and a handsome Greek Revival manor, The Oliver-Britt House.

This bed-and-breakfast inn is the creation of Glynn Oliver and Mary Ann Britt, who transformed the 1905 building into a popular tearoom and overnight lodging. The front of the inn has eight columns supporting two stories of classic Southern verandas, complete with cane-bottom rocking chairs and enhanced by tidy border gardens and shade trees. The five guest rooms offer a variety of antique, canopied, or oversized brass beds, along with ceiling fans, color television, fresh flowers, and coordinated linens, curtains, and bedcovers. Overnight guests are served a full breakfast, and lunches are available to the public Monday through Friday. On special college weekends, dinners are often served as well. A favorite luncheon dish is the innkeepers' chicken salad made with their own pickles and accompanied by their popular strawberry bread.

Mary Ann and Glynn will help guests plan the day's outings. Historic Oxford Square is within walking distance, with its many shops and restaurants.

Accommodations: 5 rooms with private bath. *Driving Instructions:* From Memphis take I-55 south to Batesville and Mississippi Route 6 east 25 miles to Oxford. Stay on the bypass and take the second exit, Old Taylor Road, left to the end. Turn right. Take the first left and go to the end. Turn right. The inn is the second building on the right.

Port Gibson, Mississippi

OAK SQUARE
   1207 Church Street, Port Gibson, MS 39150. 601-437-4350 or 601-437-5771. *Innkeepers:* Mr. and Mrs. William D. Lum. Open all year.

General Ulysses S. Grant once said that Port Gibson was "too beautiful to burn." It is fortunate he felt that way, because Port Gibson has survived as one of the state's most historic towns.

Named in honor of the many tall oaks on its grounds, this mansion is distinguished by its six 22-foot Corinthian columns imported from England and topped with terra-cotta capitals. Inside, a wide entry hall leads to a graceful staircase ascending to a columned landing, where it separates into twin stairways that continue to the second floor. The double parlor has an 1850 carved rosewood Victorian parlor suite with matching sofas, center tables, and French Rococo Revival pier and mantel mirrors. A rare Chickering piano is the focal point of the library, which is furnished with Empire and Victorian pieces.

Accommodations are in the Guest House on the grounds. The furnishings, including canopied four-poster and half-tester beds, are from the eighteenth and nineteenth centuries. A complete Southern breakfast and a tour of the mansion are included with overnight accommodations.

Accommodations: 10 guest rooms and suites, all with private bath. *Pets:* A kennel is available nearby. *Driving Instructions:* Port Gibson is 40 miles north of Natchez on Route 61.

Vicksburg, Mississippi

ANCHUCA

1010 First East, Vicksburg, MS 39180. 601-636-4931; toll free: 800-262-4822 (outside Mississippi). *Innkeepers:* May and Martin White. Open all year.

Just a few brick-paved streets away from the Mississippi River, in the heart of Vicksburg's historic district, is the Anchuca mansion. The main section of the house was built in 1830, with an imposing facade; and another story was added in 1845. This face-lift was considered rather "pretentious" in its day, although it must have appealed to Jefferson Davis, who made a speech from the new balcony during the Civil War.

Today the mansion has been restored to its antebellum elegance, complete with gas-burning crystal chandeliers, Oriental rugs, and lavish period furnishings. The original slave quarters have been transformed into guest rooms filled with formal antiques including large four-poster or half-tester beds. Two rooms have gas-burning fireplaces, and one of these has its fireplace in its bathroom. A turn-of-the-century cottage houses additional guest rooms. On the brick patio there are both a swimming pool and a glass-enclosed hot tub for year-round use. A complimentary Southern breakfast is served in the formal dining room; dinners and luncheons are catered to groups upon request.

Accommodations: 9 rooms with private bath. *Driving Instructions:* Take exit 4-B (Clay Street) off I-20 to Cherry Street and turn right. Go five blocks to First East and turn right again.

CEDAR GROVE MANSION

2200 Oak Street, Vicksburg, MS 39180. 601-636-1605; toll free: 800-862-1300 (outside Mississippi). *Innkeepers:* Ted and Estelle Mackey. Open all year.

The hills along the "Mississippi River Road" are dotted with elegant estates that are open for daily public tours. Among them is Cedar Grove, a grand antebellum mansion built about 1840 by John Klein as a wedding present for his bride. While honeymooning on the Continent, the Kleins collected lovely furnishings, many of which still grace the mansion. All the rooms have antique furnishings such as towering, canopied four-poster beds. Some guest rooms are in a cottage on the grounds. Among the modern-day comforts is the outdoor whirlpool bath near the swimming pool.

Accommodations: 9 rooms with private bath and 9 suites. *Pets:* Not permitted. *Driving Instructions:* From I-20, take exit 1A onto Washington Street and drive north to the 2200 block. Turn left on Klein Street and drive to the corner of Oak Street.

118 / NORTH CAROLINA

North Carolina

Asheville, North Carolina

FLINT STREET INNS

100 Flint Street, Asheville, NC 28801. 704-253-6723. *Innkeepers:* Rick, Lynne, and Marion Vogel. Open all year.

The Flint Street Inns are two side-by-side houses on an acre of dogwood, oak, and mountain laurel in the historic Montford district of Asheville. Flower gardens and a lily pond are in the yard. The old-fashioned houses have been restored in keeping with the early twentieth century and furnished much as they would have been in the 1920s and 1930s, including beautifully preserved overstuffed couches and chairs in the living room. A variety of Art Nouveau and Art Deco pieces are displayed, as well as a large collection of wooden clocks, all of which are in working order. Guests enjoy discovering the little personal touches throughout the inn. One guest room has a hand-crocheted bedspread, and in another, Lynne's grandmother's hat collection is hung up over the antique dressing table. A Southern-style breakfast is served in the old-fashioned dining room. The inn is centrally located just a few blocks from downtown Asheville and its restored shopping areas and Civic Center.

Accommodations: 8 rooms with private bath. *Pets and children:* Not permitted. *Driving Instructions:* Take the I-240 bypass and exit onto Haywood Street. Continue to Flint Street several blocks north of the city.

THE OLD REYNOLDS MANSION

100 Reynolds Heights, Asheville, NC 28804. 704-254-0496. *Innkeepers:* Fred and Helen Faber. Open all year.

As was so often the case in the last century, the Old Reynolds Mansion was built gradually over a period of years. The first section was constructed before the Civil War, while the third floor and porches were added early in this century. The result of this gradual expansion is a seventeen-room, three-story brick mansion on 4 acres in a country setting.

Refurbishing and decorating a home of this size has been a challenge for the Fabers, who first came to the mountain region in the early 1970s and have been working on their restoration project for more than a decade. Completed now, their home reflects Helen's decorating skills and the couple's enthusiasm for antique collecting. Wide stairways and halls have been papered with old-fashioned prints. Many windows offer views of the mountains, and the four rooms on the second floor have working fireplaces. There is also a working fireplace in the breakfast room, where guests enjoy their morning juice, coffee, and rolls. Outside, a large swimming pool built in the 1930s is surrounded by pine trees.

Accommodations: 9 rooms, 7 with private bath. *Pets:* Not permitted. *Driving Instructions:* Take Merrimon Avenue (Route 25 north) past Beaver Lake, turn right just past the stop light onto Beaver Street, and turn left up the gravel lane to the inn.

THE RAY HOUSE BED AND BREAKFAST

83 Hillside Street, Asheville, NC 28801. 704-252-0106. *Innkeepers:* Alice and Will Curtis. Open all year.

Sometime during the 1890s, Captain John Ray built this Colonial-revival home for his family. It features a wraparound porch and handsome windows and woodwork. The feeling at The Ray House is entirely English. In fact, according to innkeeper Alice Curtis, one English guest said it reminded her of the William Morris House near Oxford, England. The Ray House is furnished with a mixture of antique and reproduction pieces. Guests may use the beamed living room and the library–music room downstairs. A Continental breakfast is served in the dining room, on the porch, or in the garden.

Three guest rooms are named for famous Asheville citizens. The Thomas Wolfe Room overlooks the side garden and an ancient Japanese maple. Its bath has a built-in bookcase with books of local lore as well as paperback novels. The O. Henry Room is furnished with twin walnut spool beds, and the Bartok Room has a view of the side yard and is decorated with country-French wallpaper.

Accommodations: 3 rooms, 1 with private bath. *Driving Instructions:* From I-240, take the Merrimon Avenue exit, then take Merrimon Avenue (Route 25) north. Go to the second traffic light and turn left onto Hillside. Ray House is on the corner of Hillside and Mount Clare.

Balsam, North Carolina

BALSAM LODGE BED AND BREAKFAST
Box 279, Balsam, NC 28707. 704-456-6528. *Innkeepers:* Gordie and Marie E. Pike. Open Memorial Day through October.

On a hillside in the Great Smoky Mountains, there is a peaceful little vacation spot, the Balsam Lodge, incorporating two early 1900s buildings, one a yellow-clapboard farmhouse furnished with antiques, the other a red-and-white railroad depot moved here from town. The depot houses several efficiency apartments with a deck overlooking the mountains. The house has several cozy bedrooms and a living room where guests gather for Marie's breakfasts of homemade breads, muffins, and biscuits, set out along with pots of her jams and jellies and fresh seasonal fruits. Evenings are cooled by mountain breezes. It is then that guests often return to the living room to visit by the fireside over a cup of coffee and some of Marie's special treats. The porch, with its rockers and an old-fashioned swing, is another favorite with guests. The grounds are home to many varieties of birds and flowers, and there is a goldfish pond, complete with a waterwheel.

Accommodations: 8 rooms, 4 with private bath. *Pets:* Permitted in depot only. *Driving Instructions:* Take Route 19A-23 (Smoky Mountain Expressway) 7 1/2 miles. The lodge is approximately 1/4 mile off the main highway in Balsam, 35 miles west of Asheville.

Belhaven, North Carolina

RIVER FOREST MANOR
  600 East Main Street, Belhaven, NC 27810. 919-943-2151.
  Innkeepers: Melba G. Smith, Mark C. Smith, and Axson Smith, Jr. Open all year.

The year was 1899, and John Aaron Wilkinson had decided to build himself a mansion befitting his station as president of the Roper Lumber Company and vice-president of the Norfolk and Southern Railroad. Known for his uncompromising attention to detail, he hired a team of skilled Italian craftsmen to carve the ornate ceilings and oak mantels, and to fit cut glass into the leaded windows. The result was the largest home in Belhaven, for many years an important social center. The mansion survived intact and is today the River Forest

Manor. Purchased in 1947 by Axson Smith, who managed it until his death in 1979, the inn is now managed by his wife, Melba, and son, Axson, Jr. Still here are the crystal chandeliers installed by Wilkinson, the mahogany wainscoting and tapestries, and two baths so large they include bathtubs for two. Of the manor's eleven fireplaces, five are in guest rooms and still functioning. One walks through a grove of long-needle pines and up steps through an impressive entrance flanked by six two-story Ionic columns, to enter a house clearly of another era. The bedrooms upstairs all contain Victorian furniture, and the feeling is one of elegance, Southern style.

Jacuzzis and tennis courts are available, but many guests come to River Forest Manor solely for its food. The 75-dish smorgasbord brings guests from miles around. Among its special treasures are hush puppies, oyster fritters, shrimp creole, crabmeat casserole, homemade sausage, corn bread, roast ham and turkey, and an assortment of freshly baked desserts. The list of selections seems almost endless, and guests may refill their plates as often as they wish.

Because of the River Forest's location on the Intracoastal Waterway, guests may arrive by boat as well as by car. The River Forest Yacht Club offers sixteen-hour dock service, and marine services.

Accommodations: 12 rooms with private bath. Some are in an adjacent motel section; be sure to specify which you prefer. *Pets:* Not permitted. *Driving Instructions:* Belhaven is 30 miles east of Washington, North Carolina, on Route 264.

Black Mountain, North Carolina

THE RED ROCKER INN

136 North Dougherty Street, Black Mountain, NC 28711. 704-669-5991. *Innkeepers:* Pat and Fred Eshleman. Open May through October.

Black Mountain sits at the edge of the Great Smoky Mountains, just a short drive from Asheville, the Blue Ridge Parkway, and Mount Mitchell—at 6,684 feet, the tallest mountain east of the Mississippi River. The Red Rocker Inn is a family resort on one of the Black Mountain area's highest knobs, just a few blocks from town. The main section was built in 1894 by Silas Dougherty as a wedding gift to his daughter. A wing was added twenty years later.

Pat and Fred Eshleman took over the inn in the early 1980s, restoring it to its turn-of-the-century look with Victorian antiques. Guests often gather around the player piano in the living room, and a game room has a selection of books and games for evenings and rainy days. Meals are served in the red-and-white dining room, which has three working fireplaces. Guests may dine together around large circular tables that seat twelve or at more intimate tables for one or two couples. The specialties of the house are the Southern pan-fried chicken, fresh mountain trout, beef ribs, and chicken saltimbocca. All meals are available and are served both to guests and the public. A line of rocking chairs is set up on the veranda outside.

Accommodations: 18 rooms, 14 with private bath, and 2 suites. *Pets:* Not permitted. *Driving Instructions:* From I-40 take the Black Mountain exit (64) and drive to the center of town. Turn left, turn right after one block, and proceed to the top of the hill.

Blowing Rock, North Carolina

RAGGED GARDEN INN AND RESTAURANT
Sunset Drive, Blowing Rock, North Carolina. Mailing address: P.O. Box 1927, Blowing Rock, NC 28605. 704-295-9703. *Innkeepers:* Joyce and Joe Villani. Open May through January.

Ragged Gardens, built at the turn of the century as a summer home, is surrounded by terraced rose gardens, dogwoods, azaleas, rhododendrons, and apple trees. The building has a stone-columned entrance, and its exterior is covered with chestnut bark slabs. Inside, the inn has an unusual slate and stone staircase. Several walls have dark, chestnut wood paneling, and an interesting collection of antique ceiling fixtures has been installed throughout. The five guest rooms upstairs have wall-to-wall carpeting, comforters, and papered or painted walls with contrasting trim. Restaurateur Joe Villani, no stranger to the business, first worked at Sardi's in Manhattan, then owned The Gaslight in Greenwich, Connecticut, and later La Belle Verrière in Winter Park, Florida, and the Driftwood in Vero Beach. His classic French and Northern Italian cuisine at the Ragged Garden includes linguine al pesto, cannelloni alla Bolognese, saltinbocca alla Romana, osso bucco, and filet mignon Bordelaise. Breakfast is for guests only.

Accommodations: 5 rooms with private bath. *Pets and children under 13:* Not permitted. *Driving Instructions:* Take Route 321 into Blowing Rock. Turn west at the light onto Sunset Drive and go up the hill to the inn, across from the school.

Bryson City, North Carolina

FRYEMONT INN

Fryemont Road, Bryson City, North Carolina. *Mailing address:* Box 459, Bryson City, NC 28713. 704-488-2159. *Innkeepers:* Sue and George Brown. Open April through October.

In the late nineteenth century Captain Amos Frye amassed a fortune from the timber empire he had established in the Great Smoky Mountains wilderness. When the bottom dropped out of the lumber business in 1921, he decided to build an inn to serve the many travelers who had begun to come to the mountains as a retreat from city life.

The handsome rustic lodge was constructed of chestnut, oak, and maple timbers felled by Frye's axmen throughout his forest acreage. Frye sought out the most talented mountain blacksmith to create the inn's iron hardware, and skillful masons built fireplaces large enough to burn logs 10 feet long. One such fireplace is in the inn's lobby; another is in the dining room, where cheese soup, turkey, prime ribs, and fresh mountain trout are among the regular offerings. Breads are baked fresh daily at Fryemont, as are all its pies and cakes. Breakfast features apple pancakes, ham, and omelets.

Guest rooms are simply furnished with wall-to-wall carpeting. Windows were fashioned from hand-hewn timbers, and bedroom walls are of wide boards cut from local trees. The inn is listed in the National Register of Historic Places.

Within a short drive from the Fryemont are the Museum of the Cherokee Indian, the Oconaluftee Indian village, and the outdoor drama *Unto These Hills,* which tells the story of the Cherokee Indian. The nearby Great Smoky Mountains National Park is the most extensive wilderness east of the Mississippi. A big local attraction is white-water rafting on the Nantahala River.

Accommodations: 37 rooms with private bath. *Pets:* Not permitted. *Driving Instructions:* Take the Bryson City exit off Route 19-A. Turn right exactly 0.3 mile up the paved road at the inn's sign.

RANDOLPH HOUSE

Fryemont Road, Bryson City, North Carolina. Mailing address: P.O. Box 816, Bryson City, NC 28713. 704-488-3472. *Innkeepers:* Bill and Ruth Randolph Adams. Open April to November.

In 1895, Attorney Amos Frye built what came to be known as the "Mansion on the Hill." At the time he and his wife, Lillian, owned thousands of acres in Bryson City, and the house was designed to be fitting for a man of such property. The many-gabled mansion contains a large dining room and seven bedrooms as well as many of the original furnishings installed by the Fryes and their daughter and son-in-law, Lois and John Randolph. Today it is run as a genteel country inn by John Randolph's niece and her husband; meals are prepared in the Southern tradition. The menu changes daily and always includes salad, homemade yeast rolls, local fresh vegetables, and dessert. Entrées are chosen from a long list of Ruth's specialties, including fried chicken, prime ribs with sautéed mushrooms, stuffed mountain trout, and veal parmesan. Vegetables might be fresh string beans, squash casserole, or candied apples; the dessert of the day is often Key lime pie. Reservations are required of the public wishing to dine at the inn. A selection of mountain-made crafts, jellies, and honey is offered for sale. On warm nights guests often gather on the front porch with its country rockers; on winter evenings, a large open fireplace is kept blazing to dispel the chill.

Accommodations: 6 rooms, 3 with private bath. *Pets:* Not permitted. *Driving Instructions:* Take Route 75 (second exit) into Bryson City. Turn right at the historic sign and continue 1/10 mile.

Burnsville, North Carolina

THE NU WRAY INN

P.O. Box 156, Burnsville, NC 28714. 704-682-2329. *Innkeeper:* Betty Souders. Open all year; dining room open May to December.

At one time, an eight-room log cabin stood where the Nu Wray Inn now stands. The cabin, built in 1833, was enlarged into a full-scale country inn in 1867 by the grandfather of the current owner. The result is a Southern country inn reminiscent of many fine New England inns. It commands one end of the village square, watched over by the statue of Otway Burns. The town was named after Burns, the commander of the privateer "Snapdragon" in the War of 1812.

Having been in the same family for four generations, the Nu Wray has had time to collect and preserve a large number of antiques displayed or, more properly, used in a setting of early wallpapers and bright colonial colors. The parlor or Music Room of the inn has some of the more formal furniture, with early sofas and tufted Victorian chairs facing a grand piano in one corner. Music is clearly loved by the innkeeper, and the collection of instruments ranges from an 1830 rosewood square piano to player pianos to an early disc Reginaphone music box. The list might include even the carved cuckoo clock with its deer's head, bunnies, alpine horn, and crossed wooden rifles encircling the clock mechanism.

At the Nu Wray, the patina of time glows on an old one-armed school desk, a five-drawer chest, a deep-red harvest table, and a soft-pine hutch that holds the family collection of pressed glass and china. Some ceilings have modern tiles, but these are barely noticed in an inn that feels lived in and welcoming. As at all popular inns, it is advisable to reserve rooms in advance.

Family-style meals at long tables set with linen cloths or lace, reminiscent of grandmother's table, are served at the inn. Specialties are simple and to the point: heaps of hickory-smoked country ham or fried chicken and dressing, and plates of vegetables and salads, yams and greens, fresh tomatoes, and, of course, corn bread and baskets of buttery biscuits.

Accommodations: 32 rooms, 25 with private bath. *Pets:* Not permitted. *Driving Instructions:* Take U.S. 19 or 19E directly into the center of Burnsville. The inn is on the square. Reservations suggested.

Cashiers, North Carolina

Cashiers forms a backdrop to the several resorts dotting the countryside in this southwestern North Carolina community. To the north of the town, in Glenville, is *Thorpe Lake,* created by Thorpe Dam. The lake is a popular spot for fishing, boating, water-skiing, and swimming. This area is noted for its waterfalls, of which *Whitewater Falls,* with its double falls, heads the list. The upper falls cascade 411 feet, the greatest single drop in the eastern United States. The falls are off U.S. 64 on an unpaved road near Oakland, between Cashiers and Lake Toxaway.

HIGH HAMPTON INN AND COUNTRY CLUB

Route 107, Cashiers, North Carolina. Mailing address: P.O. Box 338, Cashiers, NC 28717. 704-743-2411. *Innkeeper:* William D. McKee. Open April through October.

High Hampton Inn, ringed by the Appalachian Mountains, is on 2,600 acres of woodland. Its extensive resort–country club offerings include horse and foot trails, a golf course designed by George W. Cobb, excellent tennis facilities, a man-made lake for swimming, trout fishing, and quiet boating, and a fine stable of horses. At this peaceful mountain retreat, guests can slip away alone to the high mountain trails or join in the many well-planned and organized activities, such as mountain arts and crafts, square dancing, and mountain clogging. The prime mover of this estate is the inn's owner and gracious host, Bill McKee.

High Hampton has a long history as a summer retreat. It began in the early nineteenth century as the summer home of the Hampton family, South Carolina plantation aristocracy. Wade Hampton III, a general in Lee's army and then a governor and U.S. Senator from South Carolina, summered here. The property was then passed on to the general's niece and her husband, Dr. Halsted, who were responsible for the beautifully landscaped grounds. The doctor bought up the surrounding farms to increase his landholdings; one such purchase led to the haunting of High Hampton. A neighboring farmer's wife swore she would die if her home was sold, and when her husband returned home from selling the land to Dr. Halsted, he found her hanging from an oak tree. According to local legend, a snowy white owl flew screeching about the dead woman's head as she hung there. To this day they say that the owls heard frequently at night here are the farmer's wife crying over the loss of the land.

Both Dr. Halsted and his wife died in 1922; High Hampton was purchased by Bill McKee's father, and began its life as an inn. The entire place burned to the ground in a fire in 1932. The present inn was built in 1933 in a rough mountain style, with handcrafted rustic furniture fashioned by local Appalachian-mountain craftspeople. The lodge is constructed of large timbers and covered with chestnut bark shingles, giving it the appearance of a much older building. The grounds around the resort have sheer granite cliffs and green mountains reflecting in the lake's crystal-clear waters. There are 130 rooms in the inn and the many secluded cottages on the estate. The cottages have shady porches, and many have the same rough chestnut siding as the lodge itself. They contain three or four guest rooms furnished with handcrafted wooden pieces and colorful hooked rugs. Each cottage's sitting room is shared by occupants of its guest rooms. There are comfortable chairs and couches and fireplaces with ample supplies of wood. The guest rooms in the inn consist of rough pine-paneling with wooden furniture and simple mountain decor. Many of these rooms also have their own fireplaces.

The inn's spacious lounge features a four-sided stone fireplace with fires in each of its hearths in cool weather. In addition to the handcrafted furnishings there are many overstuffed chairs and couches and plenty of game tables set up for guests' enjoyment in the dark-paneled room. The lower level includes a gift shop and sports-supply store.

The dining room serves hearty buffet-style meals featuring the inn's smoke-cured hams from their own smokehouse. The vegetables come fresh from the inn's gardens, and all the breads and pastries come warm from the ovens to the table. Bill McKee shares his love of fine food with his guests. Meals range from mountain fare to French haute cuisine to Southern-style cooking. There are mountain-trout dishes, a shad roe supreme, souffléed asparagus, and more. Alcoholic beverages are not served, but setups are available for guests who wish to bring their own. All three daily meals are open to guests and the public.

Accommodations: 130 rooms with private bath. *Pets:* Permitted, but must be kept in the inn's kennels (free). *Driving Instructions:* The inn is 2 miles south of Cashiers on Route 107.

Chapel Hill, North Carolina

THE INN AT BINGHAM SCHOOL

Route 54W at Mebane-Oaks Road, Chapel Hill, North Carolina. Mailing address: Box 267, Chapel Hill, NC 27515. 919-563-5583. *Innkeepers:* Jane and Bob Kelly. Open all year except Christmas week.

The Inn at Bingham School is a restored historic building that was the home of the Bingam School's headmaster in the mid-nineteenth century. Its architectural features, combining Greek Revival and Federal styles, have earned it a listing in the National Register of Historic Places. The school itself is now long gone. Set on twelve rolling acres of farmland outside of Chapel Hill, the inn consists of an original two-room log cabin built about 1791 and a wing that was added in 1801. There are period antiques throughout. The living and dining rooms, which retain their original paint and marble graining, have working fireplaces. Accommodations range from a rustic log cabin with a sleeping loft to high-ceilinged bedrooms in the main house. Four guest rooms have fireplaces, and all have modern baths, two with whirlpool tubs. English breakfasts are served in the sun room, the dining room, or on the patio.

Accommodations: 6 rooms with private bath. *Pets and children: Not permitted. Driving Instructions:* From I-85, take Exit 154 (Mebane-Oaks Road).

NORTH CAROLINA / 135

Chimney Rock, North Carolina

DOGWOOD INN

Box 70, Route 74, Chimney Rock, NC 28720. 704-625-4403. *Innkeepers:* Georgeann and Lamont Davis. Open all year.

Chimney Rock is a quaint little town lined with mountain craft shops and restaurants, along the banks of the Rocky Broad River in the shadow of Chimney Rock Park. Nearby, Hickory Nut Falls, one of the highest waterfalls in the eastern United States, drops 404 feet down a sheer granite cliff. At one end of the town, beside an old bridge, stands Dogwood Inn, where Chimney Rock looms high above, the sound of the tumbling river fills the mountain air, and the lawn stretches down to the riverbank.

The inn is most inviting with its creamy-yellow clapboard trimmed in soft blues. Rockers and hanging baskets of flowers on the decks and porches overlooking the river and mountains add to the charm. Inside is a spacious living room, with its spinning wheel, buggy seat, and grouping of comfortable couches and chairs. The cream-colored walls and staircase are hand-stenciled in blue, while the guest rooms are furnished with country-pine pieces and handmade quilts. Breakfast is served on the porch in nice weather.

Accommodations: 10 rooms with shared baths. *Pets:* Not permitted. *Driving Instructions:* The inn is 18 miles southeast of Asheville and 17 miles east of Hendersonville.

ESMERALDA INN

U.S. Highway 74, Chimney Rock, North Carolina. Mailing address: Box 57, Chimney Rock, NC 28720. 704-625-9105. *Innkeepers:* Pete and Pam Smith. Open late March through mid-November.

The Esmeralda Inn is on a hillside overlooking the mountains and Rocky Broad River across the road. Two stories of verandas span the rustic mountain retreat, built at the turn of the century and once a popular location for silent films. It was the hideout of a number of movie stars, including Clark Gable, Mary Pickford, and Douglas Fairbanks in their heyday. For lovers of the rustic country look, one step into the lobby and you know you are home. The peeled-log room features a wraparound balcony of logs held up by massive timbers, a big stone hearth, and stuffed owls and hawks perched on supports. A mounted deer head adorns one wall, and bearskins and trophies decorate others. Bedrooms, which open onto verandas or the balcony, are simply furnished, with plump comforters for color, carpeted floors, and painted board-and-batten walls, although a few rooms have modern paneling. Six chalets on the grounds are also available for guests. The dining room, with a porch that is glassed-in for cold weather, is open to the public for lunch on Sunday and dinner Tuesday through Saturday. A Continental breakfast is served to guests in the lobby.

Accommodations: 13 rooms, 7 with private bath; 6 modern-style chalets. *Pets:* Not permitted. *Children:* Under 12 inquire first. *Driving Instructions:* The inn is on Route 74, 22 miles east of Asheville.

Clemmons, North Carolina

Clemmons is the home of *Tanglewood Park* with full recreational activities open to the public. Tanglewood is 10 miles west of Winston-Salem, with its variety of historic and cultural offerings. *Old Salem,* in the heart of the city, is a restored Moravian Congregational town of the late eighteenth century and early nineteenth century. Many of the restored homes and buildings are open to the public for a nominal fee. The *Museum of Early Southern Decorative Arts (MESDA)* has many period rooms exhibiting the arts of the South from the 1600s to 1820. Green directional markers lead to the historic area and the *Old Salem Reception Center,* where the tours begin. *Reynolds House* offers an outstanding collection of American art displayed in the former home of R. J. Reynolds, founder of the Reynolds Tobacco Company. Tours of the *R. J. Reynolds Tobacco Company* and the *Joseph Schlitz Brewing Company* are offered to the public all year.

TANGLEWOOD MANOR HOUSE, LODGE, AND RESTAURANT

Tanglewood Park, Clemmons, North Carolina. Mailing address: P.O. Box 1040, Clemmons, NC 27012. 919-766-0591. *Innkeeper:* Mrs. Brenda Sanders. Open all year.

The Manor House at Tanglewood Park is the centerpiece of the 1,117-acre estate of the late Mr. and Mrs. William N. Reynolds. The park was deeded to Forsyth County by the Reynoldses, who wished to share Tanglewood's beauty. The estate was aptly described by the late Bishop Douglas L. Rights: "With the Yadkin River flowing nearby, the productive fields and orchards, flowerbeds, the ancient trees near the house and the woodland beyond, the stables and Mr. Will's racetrack, here was a delightful homeplace." The park is now a large, complete public recreation resort with rustic woodland cabins, a motel-lodge with patios and balconies overlooking wooded glens, and the Manor House itself, all offering overnight guest facilities. The Manor House was built in 1859 with several later additions and was completely renovated near the turn of the century. The house has rather formally furnished guest rooms with matching spreads and drapes of soft floral patterns complementing the pastel satins and velvets of the upholstered love seats and chairs. Several rooms have the original fireplaces, and all have views of the flowering trees and bushes around the estate.

The estate features many year-round recreational opportunities. The park provides the breeding and training of quarter horses, thoroughbreds, and show horses at the stable facilities. There is even a racetrack where the Tanglewood Steeplechase is held each May. There are also excellent tennis facilities and two eighteen-hole championship golf courses including one designed by Robert Trent Jones that was the site of a past PGA national championship. Paddleboats and canoes can be rented at Mallard Lake. Tanglewood also has a deer park, gardens, a nineteenth-century church and graveyard, and a parked train-engine to climb aboard. The park is a beautiful recreation and overnight facility in the rolling countryside just west of Winston-Salem.

Accommodations: 11 rooms in the Manor House, all with private bath, plus 18 motel units and 7 cottages. *Pets:* Not permitted in the park or overnight facilities by state law. Kennels available nearby. *Driving Instructions:* Take I-40 west of Winston-Salem about 10 miles.

Dillsboro, North Carolina

THE JARRETT HOUSE

P.O. Box 219, Dillsboro, NC 28725. 704-586-9964. *Innkeepers:* Jim and Jean Hartbarger. Open late April through October.

When the railroad came to Dillsboro in 1880, the town's founder, William Allen Dills, saw a chance to capitalize on the increasing transient population it would bring. Two years later he built a hotel he called the Mount Beulah Hotel after his youngest daughter. Over the years, many a passenger would disembark just before noon to enjoy a dinner for which reservations had been telegraphed ahead by the railroad company. In 1894, Dills sold his thriving business to R. Frank Jarrett, who renamed the hotel the Jarrett Springs Hotel to call attention to sulfur springs he had discovered in the rear of the property. After indulging in the good country cooking, visitors could now sit by the spring and sip the odorous but reputedly invigorating waters. Jarrett cured his own hams and served so much food that he offered to give a free meal to anyone asking for a refill of the meat plate. As far as is known, he never had to make good on the offer.

The traditions continue today at the Jarrett House, and heading the list are the heaping plates of food featuring country ham and red-eye gravy, fried chicken, or mountain trout, accompanied by country treats like candied apples, pickled beets, coleslaw, fresh vegetables, vinegar pie, and fresh-baked cobblers.

The inn is a restoration that was a labor of love for the Hartbargers, involving the stripping of all the paint off the original furniture throughout the inn to reveal the auburn tones of turn-of-the-century oak. The guest rooms are delightfully old-fashioned, with sheer curtains, rockers, and period beds and chests. The inn's exterior has three-tiered porches festooned with wrought-iron railings and column decorations. On the porch are rockers that serve guests today as they did seventy-five years ago.

Accommodations: 19 rooms with private bath. *Pets:* Not permitted. *Children:* Under twelve not permitted. *Driving Instructions:* Dillsboro is 47 miles west of Asheville, and the inn is at the intersection of Routes 23-19A and 19A-441.

SQUIRE WATKINS INN

Haywood Road, Dillsboro, North Carolina. Mailing address: P.O. Box 430, Dillsboro, NC 28725. 704-586-5244. *Innkeepers:* Tom and Emma Wertenberger. Open all year.

Flora and J.C. Watkins were among the first settlers of Dillsboro, where they built their large family home in the 1800s on a hillside at the edge of town. The house remained in the Watkins family until 1983 when Tom and Emma Wertenberger bought it, fulfilling a dream of becoming country "innkeepers."

The Wertenbergers have done a good job of restoring their country-Victorian and nearby carriage house, which now contains an antique and mountain-craft shop. The inn's high-ceilinged rooms are decorated with Victorian antiques, with several comfortable modern pieces in the parlor. Two guest rooms have big kitty-corner bay windows, one has its own separate sitting room and fireplace, and all have fresh flowers. Emma creates the "Squire's Special Breakfast" served in the formal dining room or in the more casual solarium. Three housekeeping cottages have working fireplaces as well. The inn is surrounded by three acres of terraced gardens. Steep stone stairs lead to the now-abandoned railroad tracks, where, in the years of whistle-stops, one could flag down a passing train.

Accommodations: 5 rooms, 2 with private bath, and 3 cottages. *Pets:* Not permitted. *Driving Instructions:* Take Route 23/19A or 23/441 to Dillsboro. The inn is at the intersection of Route 23 and Route 441 South, 47 miles west of Asheville.

Edenton, North Carolina

THE LORDS PROPRIETORS' INN

300 North Broad Street, Edenton, NC 27932. 919-482-3641. *Innkeepers:* Arch B. and Jane F. Edwards. Open all year except Christmas.

In 1663, Charles II granted the land of North Carolina to eight Lords Proprietors and their successors. The inn named in their honor comprises three adjacent historic homes, two Victorian and the other built in 1790 and remodeled at the turn of the twentieth century. The restored buildings retain many of their original ornamental trappings, such as stained-glass windows, carved-oak railings, and lacy, painted-oak fretwork in the entry hall. The rooms are decorated with coordinated colors and fabrics that complement the many European and American antiques. The Edwardses invited local antique dealers and collectors to furnish the rooms around themes representing a particular period. The results are a success down to the smallest details — the prints on the walls, the quilts and antique bedcovers, and even the pillow shams. The guest room beds, many of them graceful pencil-posters, are locally crafted. Arrangements may be made to purchase these as well as antiques used and displayed at the inn.

Guests are served a Continental breakfast of breads, rolls, and muffins baked by the innkeeper and accompanied by pots of homemade preserves and fruits. Edenton, a little Southern town on the spit of land between Albemarle Sound and the Chowan River, served for several years as the Colonial capital of North Carolina, and a number of its historic buildings remain. Guided tours of the Historic District are available. The Edwards offer special winter weekends which include tours of private historic houses and candlelit suppers.

Accommodations: 17 rooms with private bath. *Pets:* Not permitted. *Driving Instructions:* Edenton is on Route 17, between Norfolk, Virginia, and New Bern, North Carolina.

Flat Rock, North Carolina

WOODFIELD INN

Highway 25, Flat Rock, North Carolina. Mailing address: P.O. Box 98, Flat Rock, NC 28731. 704-693-6016. *Innkeeper:* Wayne and Mary Lou Smith. Open May through October.

The Woodfield Inn, which claims to be North Carolina's oldest operating inn, was built between 1850 and 1852 and has never closed, except during a thorough restoration several years ago. Under the guidance of several experts on Victorian decor, the old inn has been transformed into a splendid period inn with large bedrooms, salons, and halls typical of the era. The living room is decorated with camelback sofas and loveseats, a large crystal chandelier, Oriental carpets, ornate gilded mirrors, and antique tapestries and samplers. The entry hall and staircase walls are papered with boldly patterned prints. A large carved trunk—large enough to entomb an elephant—is set against one wall. The guest rooms and suites, some with working fireplaces, are furnished with Victorian oak furniture, decorative quilts, lace curtains, and ceiling fans. One room still has the secret opening in its floor where soldiers were hidden during the Civil War.

The dining room and sun porch are open to the guests and public for meals, where dinner entrées include steaks, chicken, prime rib, veal, and mountain trout. Two stories of latticed verandas with wicker porch furniture offer views of the sweeping lawn, tall pines, statuary, and a latticed dance pavilion.

Accommodations: 18 rooms and suites, most with private bath. *Pets:* Not permitted. *Driving Instructions:* The inn is on Route 25, about 2 1/2 miles south of Hendersonville.

Franklin, North Carolina

BUTTONWOOD INN
190 Georgia Road, Franklin, NC 28734. 704-369-8985. *Innkeeper:* Liz Oehser. Open mid-April through November.

Springtime at Buttonwood is a time of blooms displayed in profusion against the dark pinewoods into which this tiny inn is set, surrounded by dogwoods and rhododendrons. A cottage built adjacent to the Franklin golf course—between its fifth and seventh holes— Buttonwood is a golfer's paradise. Liz Oehser has furnished her inn with rustic antiques and hand-crafted items, some of which are for sale to guests. The guest rooms are in a newer wing, yet they have the same rustic appeal.

The crisp mountain air whets one's appetite, so Liz serves a variety of breakfasts to her guests. Strawberry omelets, German pancakes, and fresh coffee cake accompanied by a sausage and apple ring all make regular appearances on her breakfast table. Guests then relax on the sweep of lawn and gaze at the mountains or "work it off" white-water rafting nearby.

Accommodations: 4 rooms, 2 with private bath. *Pets:* Not permitted. *Children:* Over 10 years preferred. *Driving Instructions:* From Dillard, Georgia, take Route 441 to the outskirts of Franklin. The inn is across from the City Limits road sign.

THE FRANKLIN TERRACE

67 Harrison Avenue, Franklin, NC 28734. 704-524-7907. *Innkeepers:* Mike and Pat Giampola. Open mid-May through October.

The twenty-room, two-story inn has high ceilings, tall windows, and wide covered porches on both the first and second floors. Guest rooms are furnished with antiques, and most have lovely views of the Smoky Mountains. The decor is turn of the century, and the atmosphere is casual. All rooms have private bath and television.

The Franklin Terrace was built in 1887 as the Academy of Learning, a semiprivate academy for girls. Since completion of its restoration, the inn has been listed in the National Register of Historic Places.

The first floor of The Franklin Terrace houses an old-fashioned sweet shop, art gallery, and several antique shops. Open from 2 to 10 P.M., the sweet shop serves an assortment of pies, cheesecakes and soft drinks.

The inn is near the Cowee Valley Ruby Mines. Visitors may try their hand at mining the gems.

Accommodations: 7 rooms and 1 cottage, all with private bath. *Pets:* Not permitted. *Children:* Under 12 not permitted. *Driving Instructions:* Franklin may be reached by Route 441 from the north or south or by Route 64 from the east or west.

Highlands, North Carolina

HIGHLANDS INN
Main Street, Highlands, North Carolina. Mailing address: P.O. Box 1030, Highlands, NC 28741. 704-526-9380 or 526-9385. *Owner:* Dr. Walter Hood. Open all year.

The Highlands Inn, which occupies much of Highlands' Main Street, has changed little since it opened in the mountains more than a century ago. The sprawling white inn has rows of rockers all along the two-story veranda that stretches its length.

Today, the inn's dining rooms attract hundreds daily during the summer because of their reputation for generous helpings of country dishes and fresh seafood. The lobby serves as a lounge, with formal groupings of love seats and armchairs. Guest rooms are fresh and spotless, with white bedspreads and summery furnishings. An addition houses twelve more modern guest rooms.

The inn is ideal for those who seek a simple, old-fashioned mountain vacation away from attempts at citified elegance.

Accommodations: 46 rooms, 40 with private bath. *Pets:* Not permitted. *Driving Instructions:* Take Route 28 or Route 64 to the center of Highlands.

THE OLD EDWARDS INN

Main Street, Highlands, North Carolina. *Mailing address:* Box 1778, Highlands, NC 28741. 704-526-5036. *Innkeepers:* Pat and Rip Benton. Open April through October.

In the mountaintop town of Highlands is the Old Edwards Inn. It consists of the original wood-framed building that was completed in 1883 and a larger brick structure built in the 1930s.

Innkeepers Rip and Pat Benton, who had been searching for an old inn in need of restoration and loving care, discovered this inn, which had stood empty for eighteen years when they first saw it. They gathered up the many antiques they had collected over the years for their antique shop and restaurant in Saint Simons Island and installed them in the inn's carefully restored rooms. New wallpapers were matched as closely as possible to the faded originals still on the walls. Master stenciler Brenda Kellum applied whimsical Victorian designs to the halls and guest rooms, using animal, pineapple, and bird motifs. The guest rooms, many with balconies, have iron or brass beds or wooden Victorian sets with patchwork quilts and country curtains. The Central House Restaurant at the inn specializes in fresh seafood and hand-cut steaks.

Accommodations: 21 rooms with private bath. *Pets:* Not permitted. *Driving Instructions:* To reach Highlands, take Route 28 from the north or south or Route 64 from the east.

Lake Toxaway, North Carolina

THE GREYSTONE INN

Greystone Lane, Lake Toxaway, North Carolina. Mailing address: P.O. Box 6, Lake Toxaway, NC 28787. 704-966-4700 or 800-824-5766. *Innkeeper:* Brien Peterkin. Open May to October. Built at the turn of the century in the Blue Ridge Mountains as a retreat for the Moltz family, Greystone Inn hosted many social gatherings attended by Thomas Edison, the Vanderbilts, the Dukes, and the Fords. In 1984, the estate, overlooking Lake Toxaway, was restored and converted to a luxury resort. Guest rooms are decorated with antiques and reproductions that recapture the spirit of the earlier era. There are sixteen rooms in the original mansion, many with working fireplaces and many overlooking the water, while chalets offer additional accommodations at the water's edge.

Greystone Inn offers resort activities, including all-weather tennis courts, an eighteen-hole golf course, bass and trout fishing, canoeing, sailing, and waterskiing. An evening party boat carries guests on a shoreline cruise, and a cocktail hour is held on the veranda (guests are encouraged to bring their own liquor). Breakfast is served in the dining room, and tea is served each afternoon. In the evening, there is frequently a fire in one of the hearths in the public rooms—the library, the great hall, or the parlor—as well as in the two dining room fireplaces.

Accommodations: 33 rooms with private bath. *Pets:* Not permitted. *Driving Instructions:* From Brevard, take Route 64 west to the Lake Toxaway Estates sign. Turn left, drive 4 miles to the end, and turn right at the Country Club. The inn is past the tennis courts.

Linville, North Carolina

Just off the Blue Ridge Parkway in western North Carolina, Linville is best known as the site of *Grandfather Mountain,* one of the highest (5,964 feet) in the Blue Ridge range. A privately owned toll road leads to the *Mile High Swinging Bridge* that connects two peaks (access off Route 221). There are hiking trails, a visitor's center, and a museum of natural history. The site is open from April to November; admission is charged. Call 704-733-4337. Annual events include *Singing on the Mountain* in late June and *Grandfather Mountain Highland Games* (traditional Scottish games by more than one hundred clans) in early July. *Linville Caverns* offers a tour of the stalagmites and stalactites along a lighted underground river.

ESEEOLA LODGE

Routes 221, 181, and 105, Linville, North Carolina. Mailing address: P.O. Box 98, Linville, NC 28646. 704-733-4311. *Innkeeper:* John M. Blackburn. Open from June 1 through Labor Day.

There has been a summer lodge at this location since 1892, when an elaborate Victorian structure was built to serve the needs of summer vacationers. The original building was destroyed by fire, and the current building was erected in two stages in 1926 and 1936. Eseeola Lodge is distinguished by chestnut-bark siding and the peeled-chestnut and poplar poles that support the numerous gabled porches. With Grandfather Mountain as a backdrop and Kawana Lake just a mile away, the lodge offers guest rooms in a resort setting that includes an eighteen-hole Donald Ross golf course, eight all-weather tennis courts, a heated swimming pool, horseback riding, and an organized recreational program for children.

Most of the furnishings in the twenty-eight chestnut-paneled guest rooms were made by a woodworking shop set up by the original owners for the purpose. The beds, dressers, night stands, and other furniture are of the same chestnut as the building. The lodge was completely refurbished in 1982.

The lodge has a large lounge and a smaller lobby, both with native stone fireplaces, a card room, and a television room. The dining room serves two meals a day, with the public invited on an advance-reservation basis.

Accommodations: 28 guest rooms. *Pets:* Not permitted. *Driving Instructions:* The lodge is a mile off the Blue Ridge Parkway in the center of Linville.

Matthews, North Carolina

THE INN ON PROVIDENCE

6700 Providence Road, Matthews, NC 28105. 704-366-6700. *Innkeepers:* Dan and Darlene McNeill. Open all year.

The Inn on Providence is a three-story manor house, built as a private home in 1947, capturing the look and feel of an old Southern homestead. It is decorated with Early American antiques and fine old quilts. There is a formal sitting room, a walnut-paneled library, and a "curl-up-by-the-fire" family room. The screened-in porch, where breakfast is served—weather permitting—is furnished with white wicker.

Guest rooms are furnished with family antiques and offer views of the grounds, including rolling lawns, gardens, and cedars. One guest room has a fireplace and a canopy bed; another, a sitting area and large brass bed.

Accommodations: 4 rooms, 2 with private bath. *Pets:* Not permitted. *Children:* Under 10 not permitted. *Driving Instructions:* The inn is on Providence Road (Route 16) approximately 1 mile north of Route 51 and 10 miles south of downtown Charlotte.

New Bern, North Carolina

THE AERIE

509 Pollock Street, New Bern, NC 28560. 919-636-5553. *Innkeepers:* Lois and Karl Taylor. Open all year.

For years, Lois and Karl Taylor operated the popular Sugar Hill Inn in the White Mountains of New Hampshire. When they decided to move to the warmer climate of New Bern, they purchased the Aerie on Pollock Street, an 1870 inn with a World-War-II addition that now serves as the Taylor's residence. Guests at The Aerie have a chance to experience Northern hospitality, especially the Taylors' well-practiced New England cooking. The dining room is open to guests and the public for lunch (Tuesday through Friday) and dinner (Thursday through Saturday). Breakfast is served only to houseguests.

Rooms at the inn are decorated with Colonial and Victorian pieces as well as period reproductions. Bedrooms are each named for a distinctive decorative or architectural feature. One may stay in the Bay Window room, the Pencil Post room, or Jack's room. (Jack, the inn's winsome feline, won't bother allergy sufferers—he is just part of the decor.) A player piano in the living room often takes the lead during singalongs in the evening. The Aerie is ideally located one block from the Tryon Palace in the historic district.

Accommodations: 5 rooms with private bath. *Pets:* Not permitted. *Driving Instructions:* Take Business Route 70, off Route 70. Cross the Trent River and turn west at the first traffic light onto Pollock. Drive 3 1/2 blocks to the inn, which is one block from Tryon Palace.

HARMONY HOUSE INN

215 Pollock Street, New Bern, NC 28560. 919-636-3810. *Innkeepers:* A. E. and Diane Hansen. Open all year.

Harmony House was built between 1850 and the turn of the century, at which time the house was sawed in half and a wide hall and a staircase were added in the middle. It is now an in-town, bed-and-breakfast inn within walking distance of historic sights and a park where the Trent and Neuse rivers converge.

The inn is furnished with family antiques and period reproductions, many of which were crafted locally. Guest rooms feature mahogany pencil-post beds. The front porch has antique rockers and an old porch swing. Breakfast is served from the Empire buffet in the dining room.

Accommodations: 9 rooms with private bath. *Pets:* Not permitted. *Driving Instructions:* From I-95 take Route 70 east to Route 17, which runs through New Bern. The inn is 1 block south of Route 17, between Middle Street and Craven Street.

KINGS ARMS

212 Pollock Street. New Bern, NC 28560. 919-638-4409. *Innkeepers:* Diana and David Parks. Open all year.

Most visitors to New Bern come to tour Tryon Palace, the superbly restored governor's residence of the Royal Colony of North Carolina. Furnished with eighteenth- and nineteenth-century English and American antiques, the Palace was a center of activities leading to the American Revolution. However, the entire town is filled with handsome residences, many dating from the post-Revolutionary Federal period. It was in response to the need to provide overnight housing for tourists who appreciated early architecture that the idea of opening the Kings Arms arose.

The house itself is an interesting example of emerging American architecture. The front portion was probably built about 1847, with additions continuing until the early 1900s. A mansard roof was added then that converted its look to the Victorian period, although the front of the building remains clearly a part of the mid-nineteenth century. Inside the house, David and Diana have created guest rooms that have modern features like wall-to-wall carpeting, air conditioning, and modern baths, but that retain the original woodwork, hearths, and other architectural features of its period. Canopied, poster, and brass beds are the rule, and the decor is more of the colonial and Federal periods than of the Victorian era. Breakfast is served in the guest rooms and feature vrious freshly baked breads, biscuits or muffins. Kings Arms is within walking distance of historic sites and restaurants.

Accommodations: 8 rooms with private bath. *Pets:* Not permitted. *Driving Instructions:* Take Route 17 across the Neuse River Bridge, turn left on East Front Street, go one block, and turn right on Pollock Street.

Oriental, North Carolina

THE TAR HEEL INN AT ORIENTAL

205 Church Street, Oriental, North Carolina. Mailing address: P.O. Box 176, Oriental, NC 28571. 919-249-1078. *Innkeepers:* Harry and Frances Edwards. Open all year.

Oriental, the sailing capital of North Carolina, takes its name from the ship "Oriental" wrecked on nearby Hatteras Island in the nineteenth century. Tar Heel Inn, built in 1899, about the time the town was founded, has been totally restored and renovated by Harry and Frances Edwards, who have created an English-style country inn with herb and rose gardens, brick patios, and heavy-beamed rooms.

Inside, the public rooms are furnished with a selection of antiques and upholstered couches and chairs. There are books and magazines in the library-television room, along with a collection of jigsaw puzzles. The guest rooms have English country wallpaper and fabrics and antique or period-reproduction beds, either pencil-post, four-poster, or cannonball. Breakfasts are large country meals, with plenty of egg dishes, breakfast meats, and homemade breads. On advance notice, the Edwardses will provide dinner to overnight guests.

Accommodations: 6 rooms with private bath. *Pets and children:* By prior arrangement only. *Driving Instructions:* From New Bern, take Route 55 east to Oriental.

Pinehurst, North Carolina

THE MAGNOLIA INN
Magnolia Road, Pinehurst, NC 28374. 919-295-6900. *Innkeeper:* Leslie Wilson. Open all year.

The Magnolia Inn was built in 1896 by the Tufts family of Boston. A half-century earlier Pinehurst had been founded by James Tufts, and it operated as a private village and resort until 1971. Pinehurst continues to be preeminent as a winter resort known best for its six golf courses at the Pinehurst Country Club, where the inn has guest privileges.

The Magnolia is an imposing three-story building with a mansard-style roof pierced by many dormers. Porches are everywhere at The Magnolia, including twin porches at opposite ends of its second floor. Each porch and the guest rooms overlook the hotel's grounds and their magnolia and holly trees as well as camellias and azaleas.

The inn's twin-bedded guest rooms are air-conditioned. The living room has a large fireplace, and guests often gather here to watch television. The dining room, where breakfast is served, is bright and cheerful. The Magnolia's location facing the main street of this historic village makes it possible for guests to leave their cars parked at the hotel and walk to nearby shops and restaurants.

Accommodations: 12 rooms with private bath. *Pets:* Not permitted. *Driving Instructions:* Pinehurst is reached from the north or south by Route 15-501.

Raleigh, North Carolina

THE OAKWOOD INN

411 North Bloodworth Street, Raleigh, NC 27604. 919-832-9712.
Innkeeper: Annette King. Open all year.

The Oakwood Inn is named for Historic Oakwood, a twenty-square-block district encompassing many Victorian homes. Typical of the neighborhood is The Oakwood Inn, an 1871 house now listed in the National Register of Historic Places. True to the period, Victorian colors and papers are used throughout, and in all, there are nine fireplaces. A comfortable parlor is available to guests, as is the formal dining room where full Southern breakfasts are served. Only period antiques—no reproductions—have been used at the inn. Printed walking tour guides are available for guests who wish to explore Historic Oakwood. Parking is available at the rear of the inn.

Accommodations: 6 guest rooms, 2 with private bath. *Pets:* Not permitted. *Children:* Under 12 not permitted. *Driving Instructions:* Please call or write for instructions.

Robbinsville, North Carolina

SNOWBIRD MOUNTAIN LODGE

275 Santeetlah, Robbinsville, NC 28771. 704-479-3433. *Innkeepers:* Bob and Connie Rhudy. Open late April through early November.

Built in 1941, Snowbird Mountain Lodge is perched on the mountainside at an elevation of 2,880 feet. Constructed of chestnut logs and stone, it is small enough to be intimate (a maximum of thirty-six guests), yet large enough to have a complete dining room and to offer a variety of recreational activities. Each of the wood-paneled guest rooms is furnished with sturdy wooden beds and other simple furnishings. Two stone fireplaces are frequently fired up to dispel the chill of the evening mountain air. The main lounge has a cathedral ceiling with hand-hewn solid-chestnut beams. This room is paneled in butternut. The dining room, paneled in wild cherry, serves meals such as trout amandine, New York strip steak, and prime ribs of beef. The Rhudys take pride in their home-baked rolls, cakes, and pies.

There are miles of hiking trails through the Joyce Kilmer Memorial Forest, where guests can discover old Indian paths or, if more adventurous, climb to the nearby peaks. The lodge has shuffleboard, table tennis, croquet, horseshoes, badminton, miniature bowling, and skittles. There is swimming in a natural spring-fed pool of the local mountain stream, and fishing and canoeing in the streams and nearby lakes. White-water rafting is popular on the Nantahala River nearby.

Accommodations: 22 rooms with private bath. *Pets* Not permitted. *Children:* Under 13 not permitted. *Driving Instructions:* Take Route 19 to Topton, then follow Route 129 to Robbinsville. Follow the signs to Joyce Kilmer Forest and the lodge.

Saluda, North Carolina

THE ORCHARD INN

Highway 176, Saluda, North Carolina. Mailing address: P.O. Box 725, Saluda, NC 28773. 704-749-5471. *Innkeepers:* Ann and Ken Hough. Open all year.

The Orchard Inn is on a hillside at an elevation of 2500 feet. Its secluded 18 acres are at the end of a winding mountain drive through woodlands criss-crossed with walking paths. From the clearing behind the inn, one can enjoy vistas of the Warrior Mountain Range. In warm weather, flowers line the walk leading to the inn, and pots of hanging geraniums add color to the porch and its rustic rockers. Ken and Ann Hough have transformed their turn-of-the-century mountain retreat into an inn filled with family antiques, hand-crafted quilts, rag rugs, and decorative mountain crafts. The living room, with a fieldstone fireplace and large airtight stove, is more formal, with potted palms and groupings of wing chairs and loveseats on Oriental carpets. Bowls of potpouri, dried floral wreaths, ruffled throw pillows, and antique silver add appealing touches. A well-stocked library is tucked in an alcove, and a craft shop is housed on a porch.

The guest rooms, each with a private bath, are fancifully decorated with tiny floral print wallpapers, puffs on antique beds, and stenciled apples in some rooms. The glassed-in dining room, with its mountain views, serves breakfast to house guests and dinners to the public by reservation, all but Sunday night. The inn is in a dry county, but guests can purchase alcoholic beverages in nearby towns.

Accommodations: 11 rooms with private bath. *Pets and children under 6:* Not permitted. *Driving Instructions:* The inn is on Route 176 midway between Hendersonville and Tryon.

Tryon, North Carolina

MILL FARM INN

Route 108, Tryon, North Carolina. Mailing address: P.O. Box 1251, Tryon, NC 28782. 704-859-6992. *Innkeepers:* Chip and Penny Kessler. Open March through November.

Mill Farm Inn, on 3½ acres of landscaped grounds stretching down to the Pacolet River, is a handsome stone building constructed in 1939. Inside, guests find rooms with contemporary furniture and wall-to-wall shag carpeting. The common room has exposed chestnut beams and a stone fireplace, and off the kitchen a screened porch with comfortable furniture overlooks the yard. Guest suites have traditional furnishings such as new four-poster beds and rocking chairs.

The innkeepers, Chip and Penny Kessler, provide helpful notes on local points of interest and restaurants. Breakfast is set out in the dining room where guests help themselves. The Tryon area is famed for the natural beauty of the Blue Ridge Mountains, where a "thermal belt" results in surprisingly warm temperatures and unusually fine crops of apples, grapes, and peaches.

Accommodations: 8 rooms with private bath. *Pets:* Not permitted. *Driving Instructions:* The inn is on Route 108 between Tryon and Exit 36 from I-26.

PINE CREST INN

200 Pine Crest Lane, Tryon, North Carolina. Mailing address: P.O. Box 1030, Tryon, NC 28782. 704-859-9135. *Innkeepers:* Bob and Helene Johnson. Open all year.

Pine Crest Inn is a group of rustic cottages and a lodge in a landscaped setting overlooking Tryon from a secluded hillside at the end of a cul-de-sac surrounded by tall pines, well-manicured grounds, and little walkways leading to the various lodgings. The original buildings date back to 1906, with cottages from the 1920s, 30s, and 40s and a modern house built in 1960. Three of the guest rooms are in a pine-paneled lodge, and all rooms and suites have either a sitting room, fireplace, or both. All are spacious, with pine paneling in most and comfortable rustic furnishings combined with such amenities as air-conditioning and modern baths. The lodge houses a sitting room with couches grouped around the stone fireplace and decorative touches such as antique trunks and hunting prints. A large stone veranda is off this room, as is the dining room, which serves three meals daily to both overnight guests and the public. This paneled room is softly lit by an iron chandelier, candles set on handmade pine trestle tables, and the glow from the wood fire in the large stone fireplace. A chalkboard proclaims the day's menu, the specialties being roasts of beef, pork, and lamb, along with grilled boneless baby salmon.

Accommodations: 31 rooms with private bath. *Pets:* Not permitted. *Driving Instructions:* In Tryon, follow the sign at the railroad crossing on Route 176.

Waynesville, North Carolina

HALLCREST INN

299 Halltop Road, Waynesville, NC 28786. 704-456-6457. *Innkeepers:* Russell and Margaret Burson. Open late May through October.

Hallcrest Inn is an 1880s farmhouse near the Balsam Mountain Range in western North Carolina. At an altitude of 3,200 feet on Hall Mountain, it offers sweeping views of valleys and surrounding mountains. The front porch, with its silvery tin roof and tidy row of old granny rockers, is probably the most popular spot for sitting and enjoying the scenery. The farmhouse is set amid tall oaks, lilacs, apple trees, and dogwoods. Guests are welcome to pick raspberries, blackberries, and apples in season.

This is a very casual and homey inn. The guest rooms are simply furnished with family antiques and even come equipped with traditional creaky floors. Two rooms have fireplaces. A motel-type building houses four additional guest rooms, although we feel our readers will prefer the main house. Meals are served family-style in the dining room, which also has a fireplace. The ancient farm bell is rung to announce mealtimes and to bid departing guests "farewell and safe journey."

Accommodations: 12 rooms with private bath. *Pets:* Not permitted. *Driving Instructions:* Take U.S. 276 north from Waynesville, turn left on Mauney Cove Road; then follow signs to the inn, which is south of Route 40.

THE SWAG

Hemphill Road, Waynesville, North Carolina. Mailing address: Route 2, Box 280-A, Waynesville, NC 28786. 704-926-3119; off season: 404-875-1632. *Innkeepers:* Dan and Deener Matthews. Open Memorial Day to late October.

Almost a mile high in the Smoky Mountains, surrounded by acres of mountain meadows and woodlands, stands a mountain inn built of century-old hand-hewn logs and local mountain stone. When Dan and Deener Matthews decided to build their mountain retreat, they first had to construct a gravel road 2.5 miles long to the mountaintop. They dismantled five abandoned antique log buildings and used the salvaged materials to create an inn with nine guest rooms. Another building, Chestnut Lodge, houses a racquetball court, a sauna, a library, three guest rooms, and a living room with a stone fireplace.

The Matthewses have furnished The Swag with arts and crafts of Tennessee and North Carolina as well as with their family antiques. The living room has a cathedral ceiling, exposed-log walls, and a loft with colorful quilts draped over the railings. A player piano with several hundred rolls gets plenty of attention during the evening singalongs.

Three guest rooms are paneled in old chestnut. Six have fireplaces, and all are provided with patchwork quilts. Fresh fruit, flowers, and terrycloth robes are thoughtfully set out.

Meals at The Swag are served family style on two large tavern tables set with pewter. The entrées are accompanied by fresh vegetables, salads, and home-baked breads and desserts. The inn is in a dry county, but guests may bring their own spirits. The front porch and an old rocker offer the stillness of the mountains under a canopy of stars.

The Swag is popular for honeymoons, anniversaries, and family reunions. The minimum stay is two days.

Accommodations: 12 rooms, 11 with private bath and 4 with steam showers. *Pets:* Not permitted. *Children:* Under six not permitted. *Driving Instructions:* Take Route 276 north of Waynesville to Hemphill Road. Turn west at the inn's sign and drive to The Swag. This drive is not for the faint of heart. The road has hairpin turns and climbs nearly straight up a very steep mountain.

Wilmington, North Carolina

GRAYSTONE GUEST HOUSE

100 South Third Street, Wilmington, NC 28401. 919-762-0358. *Innkeepers:* Rodney G. Perry and D. Gordon Plummer. Open all year.

This lavish, four-story, 14,000 square foot stone mansion was the talk of Wilmington back in 1906, when Mrs. Elizabeth Haywood Bridgers commissioned architect Charles McMillan to design an Italian Renaissance Revival displaying opulent detailing inside and out. The mansion has been completely restored and decorated by two Raleigh interior designers, Rodney G. Perry and D. Gordon Plummer, who purchased the grand structure and transformed it into elegant guest accommodations. The six guest rooms on the second floor are decorated with formal antiques, plush carpeting, and original artwork. All rooms have non-working fireplaces; two have canopied beds, while another features a sleigh bed and early mahogany pieces. Continental breakfasts are served on fine china and silver in the guests' rooms. The first floor has a sitting room, a library, a music room, and a vast drawing room, all displaying fine antiques and objets d'art.

Graystone Guest House is in the heart of Wilmington's historic district, near boutiques and restaurants. The Cape Fear River is three blocks away, and a park, restored wharf areas, and the Cotton Exchange also feature shops, restaurants, and a museum.

Accommodations: 6 rooms, 4 with private bath. *Pets and children:* Not permitted. *Driving Instructions:* The inn is in the historic district of Wilmington just east of the Cape Fear River.

MURCHISON HOUSE

305 South Third Street, Wilmington, NC 28401. 919-343-8580. *Innkeeper:* Joseph P. Curry. Open all year.

Murchison House, built as a private townhouse in 1876, with several porches overlooking a formal garden and brick courtyard, is a modified Gothic structure that displays a Chippendale influence in the woodwork. The brick building, with its crisp white trim and tall black shutters flanking arched windows, is behind a wrought-iron fence in the heart of Wilmington's historic district. Each of the inn's fourteen rooms has a fireplace and modern amenities such as telephones, color-television sets, and comfortable sitting areas.

Innkeeper Joseph Curry has furnished the mansion with many pre-1840 antiques, augmenting them with period reproductions and comfortable modern seating. The library has Mission oak paneling and leaded-glass bookcases. A large breakfast is served in the formal dining room.

The inn is within easy walking distance of shops, restaurants, and the Cape Fear riverfront.

Accommodations: 4 rooms with private bath. *Pets:* Not permitted. *Driving Instructions:* The inn is at the corner of South Third and Ann streets, 6 blocks north of Routes 17, 74, and 76.

Winston-Salem, North Carolina

COLONEL LUDLOW HOUSE
Summit & West 5th, Winston-Salem, NC 27101. 919-777-1887. *Innkeeper:* H. K. Land; Mgr: Karen Clark. Open all year.

Colonel Ludlow House provides the best of two worlds, a restored Victorian home furnished with period antiques skillfully combined with modern luxuries, such as whirlpool baths for two, stereo systems complete with tape collections, telephones, wet bars, and lots of fresh flowers and greenery. The twentieth-century amenities are tucked into Victorian rooms that include half tester, brass, and carved hardwood bedsteads, Oriental rugs, and period decor. The formal parlor, dining room, and grounds landscaped with pre-1900s plantings make this bed-and-breakfast a popular spot for wedding, anniversary, and birthday celebrations. Colonel Ludlow House, listed in the National Register of Historic Places, is part of the historic West End community of Winston-Salem, within easy walking distance of restaurants, shops, and parks. The restored 1700s Moravian village, Old Salem, is just a mile away. Breakfast is the only meal served.

Accommodations: 9 rooms with private bath. *Pets:* Not permitted. *Children:* Under 11 not permitted. *Driving Instructions:* Take I-40 into Winston-Salem and take the Broad Street-Downtown exit. At the end of the exit ramp, turn right onto Broad Street. At the fourth traffic light, turn left onto West 5th. The inn is at the next traffic light.

170 / SOUTH CAROLINA

South Carolina

Beaufort, South Carolina

BAY STREET INN
601 Bay Street, Beaufort, SC 29902. 803-524-7720. *Innkeepers:* Gene and Kathleen Roe. Open all year.

The Bay Street Inn is a historic beauty. The antebellum mansion, built in 1852 in the heyday of cotton wealth by a rich plantation owner, Lewis Reave Sams, has been restored and is listed in the National Register of Historic Places. With its large white columns, high ceilings, elaborate woodwork, and fine plasterwork, the house is the epitome of the elegant Beaufort style.

The inn is at the edge of Beaufort's historic district, "Old Point," and faces the Intracoastal Waterway and the Beaufort River. Almost every window offers a view of the water. Often one can catch glimpses of porpoises frolicking below. In the distance, one can see the bridge connecting the city to the Sea Islands.

The restoration preserves the original use of each room. Hence, the Library is just that, and the parlors remain parlors complete with their black marble fireplaces. All the rooms are furnished with a variety of antiques from many periods but in keeping with the atmosphere of the inn. French, English, and American antiques are found in the guest rooms, with beds ranging from an elaborate French import to a Carolina rice bed. Each guest room has a fireplace, bath, and sitting area and all are air conditioned. Fresh seasonal flowers placed in the rooms are replaced in the off season by silk ones.

Breakfasts are served on silver, crystal, and fine china in any spot that catches a guest's fancy, be it porch, library, or garden. For beach excursions or a jaunt to the old church ruins or nearby bird sanctuary, the Roes can arrange for a picnic basket and a private tour with a knowledgeable guide. Bicycles are available for leisurely tours of this interesting Southern port. On your way in and out of the inn, take note of the cracks in the inn's marble steps. The building was occupied during the Civil War, first as an officer's club and later as a Union hospital. It is said that the cracks resulted when the ladies of the house threw trunks off the upper balcony after being warned that union troops were advancing on the city.

Accommodations: 5 rooms with private bath. *Pets:* Not permitted. *Driving Instructions:* From Charleston, take Route 17 south to Garden Corners, then Route 21 to Beaufort.

Camden, South Carolina

THE INN

1308 Broad Street, Camden, SC 29020. 803-425-1806. *Innkeeper:* John Jones. Open all year.

Camden, established in 1733, is South Carolina's oldest inland town and the scene of several skirmishes and battles during the Revolutionary War. In addition to historic sites, the area attracts horse lovers, who come to enjoy polo, horse shows, riding trails, and the Carolina Cup and Colonial Cup steeplechase races. The Inn is a complex of historic buildings with twelve guest rooms, each with a color-coordinated private bath. The inn's restaurant is located in one house and offers dinners to guests and the public. A Continental breakfast is served to overnight guests only.

Joshua Reynolds House, built in the early nineteenth century, was at one time the office of Abraham Lincoln's brother-in-law, Dr. Todd. Next door is the turn-of-the-century McLean House, which has a staircase with its original brass "dust guards" still in place. The guest rooms and parlors of both houses are decorated with a combination of antiques, period reproductions, and traditional upholstered pieces. There are several with fireplaces, and fresh flowers are the rule.

Accommodations: 12 rooms with private bath. *Pets:* Not permitted. *Driving Instructions:* The inn is just off I-20 in Camden.

Charleston, South Carolina

BATTERY CARRIAGE HOUSE

20 South Battery, Charleston, SC 29401. 803-723-9881; toll free: 800-845-7638 (out of state); 800-922-7638 (in South Carolina only). *Innkeepers:* Becky and Frank G. Gay, Jr. Open all year.

Charleston is one of the best-preserved and loveliest cities in America. Its cobblestone streets, fresh sea air, moss-draped oaks, and refined beauty of the homes, gardens, and parks overwhelm even the most jaded of all travelers. In the midst of all this is the Battery Carriage House, an ideal hideaway for visitors wishing to surround themselves with the city's gracious atmosphere. It is tucked behind a mansion built in 1845 in the heart of the historic Battery (pronounced *bah-try*,

174 / SOUTH CAROLINA

if you wish to blend in). The mansion is owned and lived in by Frank Gay and his wife, Becky, who have impeccably restored and refurbished the ground floor and Carriage House (formerly the servants' quarters) to house ten guest rooms off the wisteria-covered brick courtyard behind wrought-iron gates. The Gays' mansion looks regally out over the Battery and harbor, and its luxurious guest quarters combine the ambience of the Old South with today's modern conveniences. Out of sight behind discreetly shuttered doors are such amenities as color television, stereo radio, a fully equipped kitchenette, and a bar thoughtfully stocked with chilled soft drinks and a complimentary bottle of wine that is replenished daily. The rooms are decorated with wallpapers and fabrics of historic Charleston. There are Oriental carpets, canopied beds, and eighteenth-century–style furnishings, reproductions of the antiques that graced the many mansions and townhouses of the Old City.

A Continental breakfast of hot coffee, juice, and Benedict cheesecake (a treasured recipe of Becky's family) is served either in the guest rooms or in the walled garden shaded by wisteria vines, with potted flowers adding splashes of color from their brick-wall niches. Guests may have the use of touring bikes for exploring the city. There is also a small, heated swimming pool in the atrium. The Gays will gladly steer guests to favorite restaurants featuring Charleston's unique cuisine. They will also point out the best bike routes, museums, historic sites, and shopping areas. If guests choose to relax and stay close to the Carriage House, there is a service called Moveable Feast that delivers smoked hens, crusty French breads, fruits, cheeses, and other good things to eat. The picnic comes in a split-oak picnic basket and is delivered right to your door.

Accommodations: 10 rooms with private bath. *Driving Instructions:* Take Route 26 to the Meeting Street exit and continue on Meeting Street until you reach the waterfront. The inn is on the right.

ELLIOTT HOUSE INN

78 Queen Street, Charleston, SC 29401. 803-723-1855; toll free: 800-845-7638 (out of state); 800-922-7638 (in South Carolina only). *Innkeeper:* Michelle Baldrick. Open all year.

The original section of Elliott House goes back almost to the beginnings of Charleston. The first buildings on the property, known in 1800 as Schenkingh's Square, were erected by William Mills, father of

Robert Mills, the architect of the Washington Monument. Elliott House today has been enlarged with the addition of an eighteenth-century-style carriage house encircling an open-air courtyard. Here, period guest rooms open onto individual balconies overlooking a wisteria arbor and the Jacuzzi pool. Many guests enjoy taking their Continental breakfast out on the little tables in the courtyard by the fountain, while others luxuriate with breakfast in bed, which arrives on a silver tray with fresh pastries, chilled orange juice, and a pot of steaming coffee or tea. Afternoon tea is served in the garden.

Each room is decorated, in keeping with the inn's atmosphere, with canopied beds and handsome armoires. The latter not only hold one's belongings during a stay at Elliott House but also conceal the room's color-television set. The inn's furnishings, styled in the manner of the eighteenth century, are beautifully set off by the coordinated wall coverings and fabrics typical of historic Charleston. All rooms have telephones and daily complimentary bottles of wine.

Elliott House has bicycles for guests' use. For those who enjoy it, cycling is one of the best ways to see the many historic and picturesque sights of this lovely old city. A block to the west of the inn is King Street, the antiquing district. Going a block in the opposite direction brings one to the festive old City Market.

Accommodations: 26 rooms with private bath. *Driving Instructions:* Exit off I-26 at Meeting Street, continue south to Queen Street, turn right on Queen Street, and go half a block to the inn.

INDIGO INN

1 Maiden Lane, Charleston, SC 29401. 803-577-5900; toll free: 800-922-1340 (in South Carolina). 800-845-7693 (out of state). *Innkeeper:* Faye Neal. Open all year.

In the eighteenth century, indigo was the king of the crops, its deep elegant blue desired the world over. "Carolina Blue" was much sought after, being the finest of the Lowcountry dyes. The splendor of the era of indigo harvests has been recaptured at the Indigo Inn, a re-creation (1979) of an eighteenth-century building where lush, greenery-bedecked balconies open onto a peaceful courtyard. The emphasis of the decor is on the intensely colorful fabrics inspired by indigo dyes.

The inn's rooms feature many graceful pieces of mahogany furniture, period antiques, and reproductions. The lobby displays Oriental rugs and eighteenth-century pieces and has softly lit paneled walls. The inn's popular "Hunt" breakfast is served here buffet style on the antique sideboard. Ham biscuits are among the favorite offerings, along with three kinds of homemade bread and compotes of fresh fruit in season. The guest rooms are built around the inn's courtyard and almost all have queen-size beds. Cannonball beds and the famous Charleston rice beds are in many of the rooms.

The Indigo Inn is in the very heart of Charleston's historic district; from the inn's cobblestone entranceway, guests are but a short distance from the Market area, with its little shops, eateries, and open-air markets. The inn expanded its facilities to include Jasmine House, an 1840 antebellum, Greek Revival, building across the street, which has six suites for bed and breakfast, each furnished with nineteenth-century antiques.

Accommodations: 46 rooms with private bath. *Driving Instructions:* The inn is near the corner of Meeting and Pinckney streets.

PLANTERS INN

112 North Market Street, Charleston, SC 29401. 803-722-2345. *Innkeeper:* Perrin Lawson. Open all year.

Overlooking historic Charleston's eighteenth-century marketplace is the Planters Inn, housed in a meticulously renovated 1840 commercial structure, restored under guidelines set by the U.S. Department of Interior. The original facade, masonry, and other significant architectural details were carefully preserved, along with the columns and cornices, which were reconstructed or refurbished as needed. Within these historic walls is an elegant urban inn with the look and feel of one of Charleston's fine antebellum estates. The lobby is furnished with eighteenth-century antiques and reproductions modeled after historic Charleston pieces. The guest rooms and suites have pieces from the same period, including mahogany four-poster beds, chaise longues, and high windows draped in swags. Behind the historic exterior is a full-service hotel, with special French milled soaps, plush pillows, and nightly turn-down service that includes extra pillows and imported chocolates left at the bedside.

The inn's restaurant, Eli's on The Market, offers indoor or courtyard dining. Brunch is served on Sunday.

Accommodations: 43 rooms with private bath. *Pets:* Not permitted. *Driving Instructions:* Exit off I-26 onto Meeting Street to downtown and take Market Street. The inn is on the corner of Meeting and Market streets.

SWORD GATE INN

111 Tradd Street, Charleston, SC 29401. 803-723-8518. *Innkeeper:* Walter Barton. Open all year.

The Sword Gate Inn is in one wing of Sword Gate House in the heart of Charleston's large historic district. The main house was built in the mid-eighteenth century. In the 1820s it was used as a French boarding school for girls; and in the 1850s, as a British consulate.

The rooms, formerly the servants' quarters, are furnished simply with comfortable beds and antiques scattered here and there. Three rooms have high four-poster beds, and the fourth contains a fabric-covered bedstead. Comforters lie across the beds and coverlets and sheets reflect the changing seasons; in spring there are bright floral prints on white backgrounds, and in fall the colors are warm oranges and golds.

Charleston breakfasts are offered in the courtyard or the formal dining room. Guests help themselves to coffee, juice, fruits, and coddled eggs. Every day there are lots of sweet rolls and grits. Wine and cheese are served in the evenings.

Guests are given a tour of the ballroom, a fine example of gracious Charleston architecture. Elaborate moldings and the fireplace's carved mantels are enhanced by the ornate crystal-and-frosted-glass chandelier that hangs from the center-ceiling medallion with its gilded oak-cluster design. At the top of the house is a spacious, antique-filled bedroom with a canopied bed, its delicate top crocheted of tobacco twine. It is the honeymoon suite. Bicycles are available.

Accommodations: 6 rooms with private bath. *Pets:* Not permitted. *Children:* Under six not permitted. *Driving Instructions:* Too complicated to describe here. Get directions from the innkeeper.

TWO MEETING STREET INN

2 Meeting Street, Charleston, SC 29401. 803-723-7322. *Innkeeper:* David S. Spell. Open all year.

When Martha Williams became the bride of Waring P. Carrington in 1890, her wealthy father gave her a check for $75,000 set on a rose-colored cushion. It was to build the newlyweds a Queen Anne Victorian home. During the two years it took to build the house, known today as the Two Meeting Street Inn, the couple traveled extensively in Europe. The Carringtons donated the columned bandstand in the park across the street from the inn so that they could enjoy concerts without leaving the comfort of their piazza. They lived here for more than half a century and entertained distinguished guests from all over the world, including Princess Anastasia of Russia and Warren G. Harding before his presidency. In 1946, the inn was purchased by the Carr family and was run for many years as a guest house by Mrs. Carr, aunt of the present owner.

The inn is surrounded on two sides by arched piazzas facing Battery Park to capture the southern breezes. Standing in the large entrance foyer, one can see magnificent Tiffany stained-glass windows in the living room, dining room, foyer, and on the stair landing. A built-in china cabinet containing some of the innkeeper's collection of blue and white Canton china graces one wall in the oval dining room. Over the cabinet is a sunburst stained-glass window measuring some 6 feet across.

The inn is furnished with family antiques, silver, crystal, Oriental rugs, and period pieces. Five bedrooms branch off the upstairs foyer, and two smaller bedrooms sharing two baths are on the third floor. Three bedrooms open onto an upstairs piazza, and one of the two Honeymoon Suites has its own balcony.

The inn's corner lot has several live oak trees more than a hundred years old. A Continental breakfast is served in the dining room, on the piazza, or out in the gardens.

Accommodations: 7 rooms, 5 with private bath; including 2 suites. *Pets:* Not permitted. *Children:* Under nine not permitted. *Driving Instructions:* From I-26 or U.S. 17 exit onto Meeting Street and drive to the end of the street. The inn is at the corner of South Battery Street.

VENDUE INN

19 Vendue Range, Charleston, SC 29401. 803-577-7970; toll-free: 800-845-7900 (out of state), 800-922-7900 (in South Carolina). *Innkeepers:* Evelyn and Morton Needle. Open all year.

The Vendue Inn is a fine example of urban restoration. Evelyn and Morton Needle, with years of experience in the construction business, located a structurally sound, handsome warehouse near Cooper River. Recognizing the beauty of the old pine floors and arched windows, they set out to create an intimate inn in the tradition of Southern hospitality. The guest rooms that emerged are each differently decorated with reproductions of period furniture. There are four-postered canopy beds, brass beds, reproduction lighting, Oriental rugs, pine chests, and comfortable stuffed chairs.

The inn uses attractive linen throughout, and all the rooms have coordinated drapes and bedspreads. Each room has a complete modern bathroom, color television, and central air conditioning. Some rooms and suites have fireplaces and Jacuzzis. Beds are turned down nightly and foil-wrapped mints placed on the pillows. Bicycles are provided for sightseeing excursions. In the afternoon, wine and cheese is served in the indoor courtyard, which is festooned with hanging and potted plants. Often visiting chamber artists or members of the Charleston Symphony Orchestra play music for guests. The inn's restaurant, "Morton's," features Continental food. Vendue West is the deluxe addition to the inn, with luxurious suites of eighteenth-century furnishings and marble baths, fireplaces, and Jacuzzis.

Accommodations: 29 rooms and suites with private bath. *Pets:* Not permitted. *Driving Instructions:* Take I-26 or Route 701-17 to the center of Charleston, exiting at Meeting Street. Drive south on Meeting Street to Cumberland, turn left (east) on Cumberland to East Bay Street. Turn right and drive one long block to Vendue Range, the extension of Queen Street, which runs one way to the west.

Pawleys Island, South Carolina

SEA VIEW INN
Pawleys Island, SC 29585. 803-237-4253. *Innkeeper:* Page Oberlin. Open May through mid-October.

Pawleys Island, off the coast of South Carolina's plantation low country, is simple, unspoiled, and uncrowded. In the late eighteenth century wealthy plantation families would come here in the summer months to escape the heat. Their summer homes, surrounded by moss-covered oaks and lovely gardens, are still here. And so are the unchanged salt marshes, high dunes, and waving beach grasses.

Sea View Inn is as unspoiled as her island. It's a low-keyed family inn, a haven of uncomplicated pleasures, overlooking the salt marshes and sea. Its central courtyard takes full advantage of the ocean breezes, and the large, airy guest rooms all look out to sea. The living room is big and sunny, with bright chintz slipcovers on soft overstuffed furniture.

Sea View Inn specializes in seafood and low-country food. An evening meal might include among its many offerings a deviled-crab gumbo, black-eyed peas, and spoonbread, or scalloped oysters, corn casserole, and peach cobbler with hard sauce.

After a day of clamming, crabbing, swimming, or bird watching combined with one of Sea View's meals, what could be better than settling into one of the old rocking chairs on the veranda or strolling along the quiet beach.

Accommodations: 18 rooms with half bath and shared showers. *Pets:* Not permitted. *Children:* Under three not permitted. *Driving Instructions:* Take Route 17 south of Myrtle Beach for 30 miles.

Pendleton, South Carolina

LIBERTY HALL INN

Business Route 28, Pendleton, SC 29670. 803-646-7500. *Innkeepers:* Diane and Donelle Duron. Open all year.

Pendleton, an area of scenic beauty in the northwestern corner of South Carolina known as the "upcountry," has many buildings listed in the National Register of Historic Places. Diane and her daughter, Donelle, fell in love with the town and the 1840s farmhouse that, now restored, is Liberty Hall. The inn has a center hall, fourteen-foot ceilings, and wraparound verandas. Its rooms are furnished with Victorian antiques, and the guest rooms all have color-coordinated linens and fabrics.

The three dining rooms, open to the public for single-seating dinners, are the domain of Diane and Donelle, who offer a choice of two entrées each evening. Breakfast is served to overnight guests only.

Accommodations: 10 rooms with private bath. *Pets:* Kennel nearby. *Driving Instructions:* The inn is on Business Route 28, 1/2 mile south of Pendleton Town Square.

Tennessee

Gatlinburg, Tennessee

BUCKHORN INN

Tudor Mountain Road, Gatlinburg, Tennessee. Mailing address: Route 3, Box 393, Gatlinburg, TN 37738. 615-436-4668. *Innkeeper:* Kathy Welch. Open all year.

On a peaceful hilltop, less than a mile from the Greenbriar entrance to the Great Smoky Mountains National Park, is the Buckhorn Inn. Secluded by tall pines and shade trees on 30 acres of landscaped lawns and untouched woodlands, the inn has views of the greens and soft purples of the highest peaks of the Smokies (up to 6,500 feet).

Buckhorn Inn was built in 1938 near a spring-fed lake. In the woods around the lake are guest cottages, each with a porch, a stone fireplace in its living room, and a bedroom and bath. At the inn itself,

186 / TENNESSEE

lounge chairs line the colonnaded porch. Guest rooms inside are furnished with antiques, and each has air-conditioning and a private bath. The inn's living room is an inviting place, with bookshelves and a stone fireplace. A piano awaits musically inclined guests, and a round coffee table is drawn up to comfortable couches. Large potted plants add touches of greenery from their stands in front of the sunny windows and French doors. The dining room is set with fresh linens and candles for the evening meals, available only to guests at the inn. In winter dinner is served only on weekends.

Accommodations: 7 rooms and 4 cottages with private bath. *Pets:* Not permitted. *Children:* Preschoolers not permitted. *Driving Instructions:* Take I-441 to Gatlinburg, turn east on U.S. 321, and drive 5 miles to Buckhorn Road. Turn left on Buckhorn, drive 3/4 mile to Tudor Mountain Road, and turn right.

WONDERLAND HOTEL

Route 2, Gatlinburg, TN 37738. 615-436-5490. *Innkeeper:* Darrell Huskey. Open Memorial Day weekend through October.

Within the Great Smoky Mountains National Park is a rustic, wonderful old hotel offering an old-fashioned vacation with little to disturb the quiet but the whispering wind through the trees, the songs of birds, and the sounds of the river rushing down the Little River Gorge just 75 yards away. Built in 1912, the hotel has changed very little over the years. The wide veranda still has its row of rocking chairs where guests visit and relax, with views of the Smokies. Inside there is a large sitting area around the fireplace, a game room with Ping-Pong and card tables, and guest rooms that are simply furnished. The dining room serves three meals a day to both overnight guests and the public. Dinnertime favorites include fried chicken and country ham.

For the more energetic, the hotel provides inner tubes for floating on the river. There is a natural swimming hole nearby, and more than 700 miles of marked trails throughout the park.

Accommodations: 26 rooms, 13 with private bath. *Pets:* Not permitted. *Driving Instructions:* Take Route 441 south. Two miles from Gatlinburg, take Route 73 west and drive 4¾ miles to a sign giving directions to the inn.

Knoxville, Tennessee

THE MIDDLETON

800 West Hill Avenue, Knoxville, TN 37902. 615-524-8100. *Innkeeper:* George A. Rothery, Jr. Open all year.

In many respects, the Middleton is more like a posh private club than a luxury hotel. A small yellow canopy, a pair of old-fashioned lanterns, and a discreet sign are the only indications of the Middleton's presence—an understatement designed to attract an elite clientele.

Under its new owners, The Middleton was completely restored and decorated with eighteenth-century antiques and period reproductions. Rooms display original artwork, silver, crystal, and the innkeepers' family heirlooms. Two guest rooms have oversize whirlpool baths, and others boast sunken marble tubs, while canopied beds and chintz sofas add to the luxury. Guests are pampered with terry robes, full concierge services, private telephones, cable television, and an airport limousine service.

A Continental breakfast is served in the Hunt Room, and an intimate lounge provides an honor bar. Attention to detail, personal touches, and elegance combine to make this Knoxville hostelry special. The Middleton is next to the campus of the University of Tennessee in the city's quiet, historic Maplehurst section.

Accommodations: 15 rooms with private bath. *Pets:* Not permitted. *Driving Instructions:* From I-75 and Route 40, take the Business Loop to the Cumberland Avenue exit. Drive a short distance to Henley, turn left. Just before the Henley Street bridge, turn right on West Hill Avenue. Continue to the corner of the second block.

THREE CHIMNEYS OF KNOXVILLE

1302 White Avenue, Knoxville, TN 37916. 615-521-4970. *Innkeepers:* Alfred and Margo Akerman. Open all year.

This pretty, shingled Queen Anne mansion was built in 1896 in the Knoxville neighborhood where author James Agee once lived. The inn is encircled by the main campus of the University of Tennessee. It has four large, carpeted guest rooms furnished with Victorian pieces. Each of the guest rooms is named for a wildflower or other plant of the nearby Great Smoky Mountains region.

Guests at Three Chimneys enjoy a Southern breakfast in the glassed-in porch on the east side of the house. On warm, sunny days they may sit on the roof porch overlooking other homes of the neighborhood, many of which are listed in the National Register of Historic Places. The sloping backyard is bounded by a wall of mountain stone. A lily pool reflects a large white dogwood tree and a Southern magnolia.

Accommodations: 4 rooms, 2 with private bath. *Pets:* Not permitted. *Driving Instructions:* From Interstates 40 and 275, take exit 387 six blocks south on 17th Street to White Avenue. The inn is at Thirteenth Street.

Memphis, Tennessee

LOWENSTEIN-LONG HOUSE

217 N. Waldran, Memphis, TN 38105. 901-527-7174. *Innkeeper:* Martha Long. Open all year.

This stone mansion was built at the turn of the century by Abraham Lowenstein, founder of the Lowenstein Department Store. The four-story "late Victorian" was a showcase for the very best that money could buy: Stained glass windows, marble-walled baths and kitchen, tooled-leather wall coverings, and the finest wood and plaster craftsmanship. In the 1920s the estate was sold to the Beethoven Music Club, which held recitals in the grand conservatory room, the drawing room, and the music room, all on the first floor. It was sold again in the 1940s and, after a series of owners, fell into disrepair.

The Longs rescued the mansion and, after much hard work, opened the Lowenstein-Long House to overnight guests. It is listed in the National Register of Historic Places. The large rooms are furnished with a combination of Victorian and comfortable modern pieces. The woodwork and elaborate plaster cornices have been restored, and some of the baths retain their marble walls. A Continental breakfast is served in the dining room. In addition to the Victorian-style guest rooms, the inn has hotel-type rooms at lower rates.

Accommodations: 6 rooms, 5 with private bath. *Pets:* Not permitted. *Driving Instructions:* From I-240, take the Madison, Union, or Front Street exits to Poplar Avenue.

Pickwick Dam, Tennessee

HOMESTEAD HOUSE INN

Highway 57S, Pickwick Dam, Tennessee. Mailing address: P.O. Box 218, Pickwick Dam, TN 38365. 901-689-5500. *Innkeeper:* Gladys E. Youngblood. Open April through October.

Homestead House Inn began as the Red Sulphur Springs Hotel in 1843, later serving as both a Union and a Confederate hospital during the Civil War. Later still, the James boys, Frank Dalton, and others stayed here between bank robberies. At the turn of the century, the hotel burned and was rebuilt on a smaller scale. In 1984, the Youngbloods purchased the hotel and its 14 wooded acres and established this bed-and-breakfast inn. It is a rustic place, with pine-paneled walls and ceiling fans. Rooms are furnished with family antiques and contemporary pieces; beds are covered with quilts. Lucy Walters is the inn's baker and musician. Her strawberry bread is the highlight of breakfast. Nearby Pickwick Lake, on the Tennessee River, offers many recreational facilities.

Accommodations: 5 rooms, 1 with private bath. *Pets:* Not permitted. *Children:* Under 12 not permitted. *Driving Instructions:* The inn is on Highway 57S, 3 1/2 miles south of Pickwick Dam.

Red Boiling Springs, Tennessee

DONOHO HOTEL

East Main Street, Red Boiling Springs, Tennessee. Mailing address: P.O. Box 36, Red Boiling Springs, TN 37150. 615-699-3141. *Innkeepers:* Patrick and Edith Walsh. Open May through September.

Red Boiling Springs had its heyday in the Roaring Twenties when people flocked from all over to partake of the cure-all waters of the springs. At that time there were eight or nine hotels and numerous tourist homes serving the health-seeking tourists. Despite this, many visitors could not be accommodated and had to sleep in their cars. Several of these hotels burned over the years, including one with the rather cheerless name of Deadman Hotel.

Unlike its peers, the Donoho Hotel is still going strong today, in spite of a definite decline in the tourist trade about town. Built in 1914, it is a traditional old-fashioned summer resort hotel with a long, colonnaded two-story porch, complete with comfortable rocking chairs. Tall shade trees grace the lawn where wooden lawn chairs are arranged. Many of the area's attractions remain, including its lovely lakes, a golf course, a swimming pool, and tennis courts in the village.

Innkeeper Edith Walsh confides, however, that the main attraction at the Donoho is its big front-porch rockers where, after a good meal in the hotel dining room, folks simply like to sit, talk, and rock while waiting for the next mealtime to roll around.

There is every reason for anticipation concerning meals. The Donoho is famous for its no-menu, family-style, all-you-can-eat dining. The big dinner bell rings three times daily, at 8 A.M., noon, and 5 P.M. At lunch and dinner each table in the old-fashioned dining room is filled with large bowls of a variety of vegetables and large plates of country ham, fried chicken, or roast beef. Heaps of hot homemade biscuits accompany the meal, and pots of honey and preserves are always on hand. The bowls and platters are refilled as needed until the meal is over. The dining room is open to the public, but reservations are advised. For houseguests, two or three meals daily are included in the room rate.

Inside the hotel, one is transported back in time to a gentler era when the pace was slower. Ceiling paddle-fans still lazily push the air about, and hand-painted shades adorn the hanging lamps in the public rooms. Downstairs are a gift shop, a lobby, and a music room containing the hotel's television and piano. Guest rooms here are simply yet comfortably furnished with antique pieces as well as traditional summer hotel furniture.

Guests who wish to sample one of the three kinds of mineral waters at Red Boiling Springs (there used to be five) need only stroll across the wooden footbridge spanning Salt Lick Creek.

Accommodations: 44 rooms, 36 with private bath. *Driving Instructions:* From Lafayette, take Route 52 to Red Boiling Springs.

Rogersville, Tennessee

HALE SPRINGS INN

Town Square, Rogersville, TN 37857. 615-272-5171. *Innkeepers:* Mr. and Mrs. Stan Pace. Owners: Captain and Mrs. C. Netherland-Brown. Open all year.

The historic little town of Rogersville in the hills of eastern Tennessee was founded in 1786 on land that was a wedding gift to Joseph Rogers and his bride. Davy Crockett's grandparents had a cabin on Crockett Creek, which runs through town, and the Crocketts and the Rogerses are all buried in the old town cemetery. In 1824, Hale Springs Inn was built on Main Street and has been in business ever since, making it the oldest inn in continuous operation in Tennessee. In the Civil War it served as the Union headquarters. Andrew Jackson lived in the hotel for a spell, and over the years it was visited by two more presidents.

It was only natural someone would come along and tackle the renovation of this historic inn. That someone was Carl Netherland-Brown, previously a captain of the liner SS Bahama Star, who purchased the inn and undertook its restoration. The oldest section is furnished with antiques and rugs of the early nineteenth century, and wallpapers were found that approximate those of the period. Most guest rooms have fireplaces; some, four-poster beds.

The dining room is decorated with Colonial furnishings and has two working fireplaces. Candlelight meals are served to the public, with roast beef the house specialty. Hawkins County is dry, so guests should bring their own spirits.

Accommodations: 10 rooms with private bath. *Driving Instructions:* Rogersville is halfway between Knoxville and Bristol on Rt 11 W.

Rugby, Tennessee

HISTORIC RUGBY

Highway 52, Rugby, TN 37733. 615-628-2441 or 628-2269. Open all year except 2 weeks at Christmas.

Rugby, a tiny English-style hamlet, is in the heart of Tennessee's Cumberland Mountains. In 1966 area residents banded together to restore and preserve this historic town, which was founded in 1880 by English author and social reformer Thomas Hughes. He designed and built this community as a cultural cooperative where he felt that young Englishmen in America could channel their energies into agricultural and manual trades. The community was carefully planned with parks, lawn tennis, and about seventy Victorian buildings. Rugby prospered for a few short years; but severe winters, a typhoid epidemic in 1881, and the tendency of the young men to prefer cultural events and high tea to work all contributed to the demise of Hughes's dream.

Although many of the original buildings burned in the last century, today the townspeople are dedicated to the restoration of the remaining buildings and the reconstruction of others. Guided walking tours of historic buildings are conducted daily, March through mid-December. Pioneer Cottage, built in 1880 as the first frame house in Rugby, has been restored and is now available to overnight guests. Newbury House Inn was Rugby's first "public house." A nice counterpoint to the more rustic Pioneer Cottage, it has been restored and furnished with more formal Victorian pieces. Guests are served evening tea in the 1880 parlor with its ceiling fans, fireplaces, and Victorian library. The Harrow Road Cafe offers Cumberland Plateau and British specialties all year.

Accommodations: 8 rooms, 3 with private bath. *Pets:* Not permitted. *Driving Instructions:* Historic Rugby is on Route 52, about 60 miles northwest of Knoxville.

Texas

Austin, Texas

SOUTHARD-HOUSE
908 Blanco, Austin, TX 78703. 512-474-4731. *Innkeepers:* Rejina, Jerry, and Kara Southard. Open all year except two weeks in August.

This recent addition to Austin's bed & breakfast scene was built in the late 1890's. About ten years later, the owners decided to enlarge the house by raising the entire structure in the air and constructing a new floor below. One of the first women journalists in Texas, Dorothy Luttrell, lived in the house in 1912. Following a flood in the 1930s, a spring in the inn's cellar provided fresh drinking water for many Austin residents whose wells had been contaminated.

Southard-House opened as an inn subsequent to an extensive renovation in 1985-86. It has four guestrooms and a two-room fireplace suite that sleeps four. Antique furnishing are the rule, including marble-topped sinks, clawfooted tubs, iron-and-brass beds, and period wardrobes. An upstairs porch has a hammock.

Breakfasts of fresh fruit, home-baked breads, and coffee are served

EAST
TEXAS

in the dining room or, in warm weather, in the courtyard gazebo. The inn is just three blocks from restaurants, shops, and galleries.

Accommodations: 4 rooms and one suite, all with private bath. *Pets and young children:* Not permitted. *Driving Instructions:* From I-35 take the Sixth Street Exit. Drive west on Sixth to Blanco, turn north, and drive to the inn at 908 Blanco.

Bastrop, Texas

THE PFEIFFER HOUSE

1802 Main Street, Bastrop, TX 78602. 512-321-2100. *Innkeepers:* Charles and Marilyn Whites. Open all year.

The town of Bastrop recently celebrated its 150th birthday, making it one of the oldest villages in Texas. It is a small, sleepy place, with many fine old houses set along shady streets, an old-fashioned drug store complete with soda fountain, and a vintage 5¢ & 10¢ store. Just down Main Street, on a large corner lot flanked by several big shade trees, is the Pfeiffer House, a gingerbread Victorian "Carpenter Gothic" built in 1901, now listed in the National Register of Historic Places. The Whites are proud of their home and have opened its antique-filled rooms to overnight guests. Bedrooms include handmade quilts, fruit baskets, homemade cookies set out on a tray, and bouquets of fresh flowers. One room has a half-tester bed and a sitting area. Charles and Marilyn make guests feel right at home, inviting them to use the inn's several public rooms, which are filled with books, bric-a-brac, and more family antiques. A full breakfast is served in the dining room. Out in the yard, the clucking sounds of chickens and the buzz of hummingbirds belie the inn's town location.

Accommodations: 3 rooms with shared baths. *Pets and children under 10:* Not permitted. *Driving Instructions:* From Austin, take Route 71 east. Take Business Loop 150 directly to Main Street. The Pfeiffer House is seven blocks north.

THE PINK LADY

1307 Main Street, Bastrop, TX 78602. 512-321-6273. *Innkeeper:* Jerry R. Wagoner. Open all year.

The Pink Lady is an 1890 Victorian gingerbreaded cottage on a spacious tree-shaded lot. The house and its guest house out back are enclosed by a white picket fence. The buildings are painted pink, with white Eastlake trim on the verandas and eaves. Rooms are carpeted and furnished with country pine and more formal Victorian hardwood pieces, although a sitting room is more contemporary in style. Breakfast is served here, overlooking the brick patio.

The guest rooms, with 14-foot ceilings and white-shuttered windows, have coordinated fabrics and wall coverings set off by formal Victorian furnishings. The cottage, with more informal country antiques, has a painted, stenciled floor, wainscotting, and a painted, antique iron bed.

Accommodations: 5 rooms with private bath; 1 cottage. *Driving Instructions:* From Austin, take Route 71 east; follow Business Loop 150 to Main Street in Bastrop. The inn is north of town.

Bellville, Texas

HIGH COTTON INN

214 South Live Oak, Bellville, TX 77418. 409-865-9796. *Innkeepers:* George and Anna Horton. Open all year.

High Cotton Inn is a 1906 house with a two-story veranda and porch swings in a small-town setting sixty-five miles west of Houston. Anna and George Horton live on the ground floor of their inn, with "three resident house cats, one house dog, and one house kid." The inn is decorated with Victorian antiques and period-style wallpapers, and the sitting room always has a well-stocked cookie jar. The Hortons have a late-afternoon get-together and serve complimentary cheeses and wines to those assembled in the kitchen. Breakfast is served to guests each morning; lunches and dinners are available to groups of at least ten by reservation only. The one-entrée, *prix fixe* dinners are served family-style to guests and the public around an antique mahogany dining-room table that can seat up to twenty-four. Guests are welcome to help out in the garden or just curl up on the veranda and, along with the cats, keep an eye on the town.

Accomodations: 5 rooms with shared bath. *Pets:* Not permitted. *Smoking:* Not permitted. *Driving Instructions:* Take Route 36 into Bellville, where it becomes Live Oak.

Big Sandy, Texas

ANNIE'S BED AND BREAKFAST

Highway 155 North, Big Sandy, Texas. Mailing address: P.O. Box 928, Big Sandy, TX 75755. 214-636-4355. *Innkeeper:* Robin Ham. Open all year.

Annie's Bed and Breakfast is part of a Big Sandy empire. Many readers may be familiar with Annie's Attic, a thriving mail-order needlepoint business. In addition, there is Annie's Tea Parlor, a popular restaurant; Annie's Gift Shop, offering turn-of-the-century items; and Annie's Needlepoint Gallery, a showcase of the craft items available from Annie's Attic. The bed-and-breakfast inn is located in the Tohill House, a seven-gabled, Victorian-style building with spindle-and-lattice enclosed, upper-and-lower-story porches, deep green lawns, and a profusion of blooms in the gardens bordering the house. One guest room, the Queen Victoria room on the main floor, has a richly hued Oriental rug, antique armoire, brass bed topped with a red satin comforter, and a handsome mantel surrounding the fireplace. Upstairs, the Queene Anne room is an attic suite with its own spiral staircase leading to a loft, red wall-to-wall carpeting, and a quilt over a hand-crocheted bedspread, both from the Annie's Attic. Guests may have all their meals, if they wish, right across the street at Annie's Tea Room, which offers Continental and complete breakfasts, luncheons, and dinners that include prime ribs, roast tenderloin of beef, Alaskan salmon, and chicken Florentine. Desserts are a specialty, especially the white chocolate mousse and "mystery" pecan pie.

Accommodations: 13 guest rooms, 8 with private bath. *Pets and smoking:* Not permitted. *Driving Instructions:* Take Route 155 north of I-20 to Big Sandy, just off U.S. Route 80.

Castroville, Texas

LANDMARK INN STATE HISTORIC SITE
U.S. 90 and Florence Street, Castroville, Texas. Mailing address: P.O. Box 577, Castroville, TX 78009. 512-538-2133. Open all year; park hours: 8–8.

The Landmark Inn is a venerable Texas inn owned by the Texas Parks and Wildlife Department, which operates it as a functioning inn within the setting of a state park. Erected in three sections from 1848 to 1870, the Landmark Inn reflects the cultural heritage and tradition of its builders, immigrant settlers from Alsace-Lorraine. The buildings resemble European Alsatian farmhouses with uniquely Southwestern architectural variations. All are built of native limestone and have 15- to 18-inch plastered walls. The banister of the stairs leading to the upper balcony is made of one continuous piece of cypress. A detached bathhouse had a lead-lined upper story that was used to provide hot baths for guests in the 1850s. According to tradition, the lead was melted into Confederate bullets during the Civil War. From 1867 to 1870, the large downstairs room with hand-hewn doors of pecan wood was the Castroville post office. Slots for mail may still be seen in the doors. The inn's Room 5 served as the Western Union office when cotton was the area's major crop. Most of the guest rooms are adjacent to the upper gallery of the original hotel and overlook a landscaped courtyard and the old Grist Mill that is part of the historic site. The stone buildings filter out highway sounds and create a tranquil atmosphere. Perhaps this tranquillity attracted Robert E. Lee to the inn as a guest a century ago. In restoring the guest rooms, care was taken to make good use of the inn's collection of Texas antiques. The state bought furnishings that would reflect the various ownerships of the inn through the years.

Park property surrounding the Landmark Inn is open to the public for tours and includes a collection of Alsatian-style buildings that reflect the area's many French-Alsatian settlers. Other Alsatian buildings of interest include the Lutheran Youth Building, constructed in 1849 as a store; the Carle House and store; the Nicholas Haby House; and the Keifer House (1870). Many of these pioneer homes are open during the spring in even-numbered years.

Accommodations: 8 rooms, 4 with private bath. *Pets:* Not permitted. *Driving Instructions:* Travel west on Route 90, turning left immediately after crossing the Medina River in Castroville.

Eagle Lake, Texas

THE FARRIS 1912

201 North McCarty Avenue, Eagle Lake, TX 77434. 409-234-2546. *Innkeepers:* William and Helyn Farris. Open all year except the first two weeks of July.

The year 1912 was part of the golden age of Eagle Lake, a time that saw the town bustling with travelers who had converged there via three railways. Today the town is quieter and is known as the "goose-hunting capital of the world." It was in 1912 that the Farris was built, and all of its furnishings are from that era or earlier. The lobby and parlors contain a mix of white wicker pieces and more formal upholstered Victorian chairs and settees. Green plants and flowers abound, and paddle fans turn gently on warm days. The sixteen guest rooms in the main building have fancy iron beds, high-back oaken beds, and older Victorian four-posters. The Governor's Suite has a canopied bed. Most bedrooms have patchwork spreads, lace curtains, and frilly dust ruffles. For guests who prefer a separate building with first-floor rooms, there is a detached 1920s guest house where most furnishings date from the early twentieth century.

During the winter hunting season, the inn serves three meals a day to guests and the public. Food is available the rest of the year when the guest load warrants. House specialties include pork chops with cherry sauce, coq-au-vin, plum bread pudding, and pecan pie. Both Farris buildings stand behind tall Spanish gates. Within the courtyard is a large carved stone fountain, near which are outdoor tables and chairs.

Accommodations: 24 rooms, 8 with private bath. *Pets:* Not permitted. *Children:* Under twelve permitted in guest house only. *Driving Instructions:* From I-10 take exit 720 at Sealy. Drive south 1 mile to FM 3013, and continue on that road to Eagle Lake.

Fayetteville, Texas

COUNTRY PLACE HOTEL
"On the Square," Fayetteville, Texas. Mailing address: P.O.Box 211, Fayetteville, TX 78940. 409-378-2712. *Innkeeper:* Jean Barret. Open all year.

Fayetteville (population 400) is in the heart of Texas's "bluebonnet country," where every April millions of wildflowers blanket the ground. Since the turn of the century, the Zapp Building has stood beside the village square here. In its long career it had served as a department store, a hospital, and a boardinghouse for drummers. Today, the second-floor corner balcony room serves as the hotel's parlor. This room is airy with refreshingly spare furnishings: antique wicker and unadorned arched windows overlooking the square. The hotel has two second-floor verandas, one running across the front and the other overlooking a little garden out back with a fountain. A few village skeptics, informing visitors about the hotel, will thoughtfully warn that the furnishings are "kind of old." The "kind of old" furniture is an eclectic blend of old-fashioned pieces, some Victorian carved walnut beds and bureaus and others painted in keeping with the hotel's age. All the beds are covered with handmade patchwork quilts, and even the "air conditioning" is old-fashioned—big old paddle fans overhead.

On the ground floor is the hotel's restaurant, Country Place, which is open to the public. Innkeeper-chef Jean Barret serves Continental fare for Friday and Saturday dinner and Sunday brunch, with breakfast on Saturdays and Sundays only. There are several cafés in town for meals not offered by the hotel. The Country Place Hotel is a recreation of a bygone institution—the old drummer hotel of the kind once found in many railroad towns across the country.

Accommodations: 8 rooms with 2 hall baths. *Driving Instructions:* The hotel is midway between Austin and Houston, 6 miles north of Route 71.

THE LICKSKILLET INN

Fayette Street, Fayetteville, Texas. Mailing address: P.O. Box 85, Fayetteville, TX 78940. 409-378-2846. *Innkeepers:* Steve and Jeanette Donaldson. Open all year.

The Lickskillet Inn and the tiny Texas town of Fayetteville appear to be unchanged by the years. But the house, built in 1852 just off the town square, has undergone some updating since its early days. For one thing, its old central "dog run"—the equivalent of an Easterner's breezeway—is now enclosed and doubles as a hallway and a display area for the Donaldsons' many antiques. Just off the "run" are the inn's guest rooms. Each is decorated with antiques and has many appealing personal touches such as crocheted doilies, knick-knacks, and perhaps an old hand mirror or someone's well-loved doll. The rooms have paddle fans, pot-bellied stoves that the Donaldsons will light on cool evenings, and antique beds covered with quilts and crocheted pillow shams. Guests are told the rules of the house when they arrive: Wet towels in the hamper, no smoking, fragile quilts in the armoire at night, and first one up plugs in the coffeepot. Innkeepers and guests eat together in the dining room, where guests are served homemade breads with jams and local honeys with their meals. Jeanette Donaldson is well versed in local lore and enjoys helping people plan their day's explorations.

Accommodations: 4 rooms with shared bath. *Pets, smoking, and children:* Not permitted. *Driving Instructions:* Fayetteville is 15 miles east of La Grange on Route 159.

Fredericksburg, Texas

BARON'S CREEK INN

110 East Creek Street, Fredericksburg, TX 78624. 512-997-9398.
Innkeepers: The Switzer family. Open all year.

Fredericksburg, founded by German immigrants in 1848, has many stone homes and buildings, along with festivals and shops. Baron's Creek Inn is on a quiet side road surrounded by lawns and stone walls. Behind the turn-of-the-century main house is a grape arbor, a goldfish pond, and the tiny "Sunday House," now a guest cottage with 1940s-style furnishings, a living room, and a kitchen–dining room. The inn and the cottage have been completely restored.

Guest suites are furnished with country-Victorian antiques and lace curtains. Each has a living room with a convertible couch, a bedroom, a kitchen–dining room, and an old-fashioned bathroom with unusual brass fixtures. Breakfasts are brought to the suites, while Texas wines and cordials are served in the evening. The Switzers also own and operate a vineyard outside of town and a restaurant and wine bar in Fredericksburg.

Accommodations: 2 suites; 1 cottage. *Driving Instructions:* Take Route 290 to Main Street. Turn south on Llano Street and west on Creek Street.

Galveston, Texas

THE VICTORIAN INN

511 Seventeenth Street, Galveston, TX 77550. 409-762-3235. *Innkeeper:* Yvonne Hern Daniel. Open all year.

In 1899, Isaac Hefron built one of the most striking homes in Galveston. Its bright white and rust-red exterior has three separate balconies and a curved wraparound porch. The superior craftsmanship Hefron insisted on is well preserved in the interior. Five fireplaces boast carved oak mantels and are inset with Belgian tiles. Stair railings show skillful carving, and much of the inn's original stained glass is still intact.

Spacious guest rooms have been individually decorated with a variety of antique pieces, which were chosen for their particular appeal rather than to create the mood of a particular historical period. One room has a tall antique armoire; two others have fireplaces; and all have king-size brass beds. Each room is air conditioned and either shares a balcony or has its own. The suite has its own sitting room and private bath. A Continental breakfast is served in the dining room.

Accommodations: 4 rooms with shared baths; 1 suite. *Pets:* Not permitted. *Children:* Under twelve not permitted. *Driving Instructions:* Take I-45 into Galveston, where it becomes Broadway. Turn left on Seventeenth Street and drive five blocks to the inn.

Granbury, Texas

THE NUTT HOUSE
 Town Square, Granbury, TX 76048. 817-573-5612. *Innkeeper:* Madge Peters. Open all year.

The Nutt House has been offering Texas country cooking for many years. Now, to the joy of travelers, guest rooms on the second floor have been opened so that they can rise from the groaning board and go straight upstairs for a good night's sleep. Most of the rooms share bathrooms, but the nostalgia more than makes up for the short walk down the hall. Each of the rooms, which once were used by traveling salesmen, has hot and cold running water and ceiling fans. Old dressers and iron bedsteads add to the turn-of-the-century look. Madge has added another historic old house to this inn, offering four additional antique-furnished rooms with private baths.

The Nutt House was built in 1893 as a store operated by the Nutt family. Downstairs, in the dining rooms, guests and the public can sit down to a buffet meal. Dinner is served Tuesday through Friday from 11:30 to 2:00 and on weekends from 11:30 to 3:00. Supper is offered on Fridays and Saturdays only, from 6:00 to 8:00. The dining room serves regional foods of early Texas. In this region, this does not mean steak every day. The pioneers took foods familiar to them and added special touches unique to the Southwest. Among the many regional specialties are chicken and dumplings, beef pot pie, meat loaf, and sliced ham—all served with grits and gravy. Accompanying these dishes are pots of beans, homemade chow chow, and tiny rounds of fried hot-water cornbread. Save room for dessert: Hot peach cobbler or buttermilk pie.

Accommodations: 15 rooms, 5 with private bath, and 3 apartments.
Driving Instructions: Take Route 377 southwest from Fort Worth.

Houston, Texas

LA COLOMBE D'OR
3410 Montrose Boulevard, Houston, TX 77006. 713-524-7999. *Innkeeper:* Stephen N. Zimmerman. Open all year.

La Colombe d'Or is billed as "Houston's finest and only European chateau," paying homage to the famed *auberge* of the same name in St. Paul-de-Vence, France. Innkeeper Stephen Zimmerman has long admired the casual elegance and impeccable service of the French version, and he set out to create its counterpart in the United States.

The 21-room mansion was built in 1923 by Exxon's founder Walter Fondren for his family. It is set on landscaped grounds in the fashionable Montrose section of Houston, just minutes from the city's "magic circle" and the Galleria. Except on Sunday, the mansion offers French cuisine in attractive antique-filled dining rooms ensconced in the former music room and parlor. Wines, including ports and sherries, as well as traditional cocktails, are served in the library, which has the atmosphere of an English club. Upstairs are several guest suites.

One suite, the Cézanne, is decorated in deep greens with rich tomato-colored accents. Its dining room overlooks the treetops and has a carved walnut table, chairs, and sideboard. The Renoir suite, a favorite, has a *Chinoise* theme with an antique carved headboard inlaid with ivory, lacquered chests, and a colorful cloisonné table. Visitors craving extra-special pampering can find no better place.

Accommodations: 5 suites with private bath. *Pets:* Not permitted. *Driving Instructions:* From I-45 take Main Street south to Westheimer Road. Turn right on Westheimer and then left on Montrose.

Jefferson, Texas

EXCELSIOR HOUSE
211 West Austin Street, Jefferson, TX 75657. 214-665-2513. *Innkeeper:* Carol Wetsel. Open all year.

Running the length of the front of Excelsior House is a gallery supported by ten iron posts, on top of which is a decorative iron railing. The hotel's Victorian ambience unfolds at the opening of its doors. In the golden days of Jefferson's past, the distinguished guest list included Ulysses S. Grant, Rutherford B. Hayes, Diamond Bessie, railroader Jay Gould, and Oscar Wilde. Today's Excelsior is no less fit to entertain presidents, thanks to the Jesse Allen Wise Garden Club, a group devoted to restoring historic Jefferson.

The hotel is a masterpiece of Southern restoration, with period antiques of maple, cherry, and mahogany, all with the warmth and patina of age. Oriental rugs lie on richly colored wood floors, the pressed-tin and plaster ceilings are freshly painted, portraits cover the walls, and swagged drapes frame each window. Some of the furniture is of museum quality, such as the marble-topped Belter table in the ballroom or the flat-topped ceiling-height canopied bed (complete with tufted canopy cover). Equally distinctive are the sleigh and Jenny Lind spool beds in other guest rooms. The Excelsior is devoted to chandeliers, with a crystal one in the ballroom and an ornate brass and porcelain fixture from Dresden hanging in the dining room. Each of the guest rooms is special, with furnishings that complement its beds. In the morning, guests gather for a groaning-board Southern breakfast, the only meal served in the hotel.

The Excelsior is definitely worth the trip. Jefferson is a transition from the Texas bayous to its cattle country to the west and south. Texas is a big state, and the Excelsior is a fine place to rest up before pushing onward to see more.

Accommodations: 14 rooms and 2 suites with private bath. *Pets:* Not permitted. *Driving Instructions:* Take Route 59 to the center of Jefferson.

HOTEL JEFFERSON

124 West Austin Street, Jefferson, TX 75657. 214-665-2631. *Innkeepers:* Nele and Tanya Plumb. Open all year.

In the 1850s and 1860s up to fifteen steamboats could be seen lined up at Jefferson's docks. Iron ore had been discovered nearby and a thriving pine, cypress, and cotton industry kept more than 30,000 persons financially secure in the town. Many tons of baled cotton were stored each year in the two-story brick warehouse on West Austin Street, which was built in 1861. And well built it was, with a laid-up-brick pyramid foundation that tapered from almost 8 feet at the base to the 18-inch walls of the warehouse itself. By 1900, the town's population had dwindled along with the river traffic because the railroad industry had bypassed Jefferson. That year, the warehouse was converted into a hotel. It has recently undergone a restoration under the supervision of owner-innkeepers Nele and Tanya Plumb.

The lobby of the hotel and many of the downstairs rooms have birch-paneled wainscoting. Also in the lobby are the original wicker couches and chairs. The guest rooms, most of which are on the top floor, have an old-fashioned look preserved through the use of antique brass, high-back Victorian and decorative iron beds, complemented by oak and marble-topped dressers, old rockers, and straight chairs. Other rooms have queen-size, newer brass beds but retain the older accessory furniture. Four of the bathrooms upstairs have clawfooted tubs, while the others have more modern fixtures or showers. Some of the guest rooms still have the original ceiling fans.

The dining room at the Jefferson offers breakfast and lunch Tuesday through Sunday, and dinners on Friday and Saturday only. The menu for all meals is à la carte, with a full "plantation" breakfast available. Luncheon specials often include Swiss steak, roast beef, baked ham, or chicken cacciatore on spaghetti. The weekend dinners include several steaks, a bacon-wrapped chopped sirloin, shrimp gumbo, fried shrimp, fried oysters, seafood platters, and boiled shrimp.

Accommodations: 22 rooms with private bath. *Pets:* Not permitted. *Driving Instructions:* Take Route 59 to the center of Jefferson.

PRIDE HOUSE

409 Broadway, Jefferson, TX 75657. 214-665-2675. *Innkeeper:* Ruthmary Jordan. Open all year.

The Pride House is a Victorian gingerbread guest house. There are stained-glass windows in every room, the original ornately decorated brass hardware on the five-paneled doors, and exceptional millwork and cabinetry throughout. The house was built by G. W. Brown, a sawmill owner, in 1889. He evidently used his finest hardwoods in the construction, and the three layers of thick wood wreaked havoc on the restorers' saws and drills. Fine woodwork can be seen in the beaded wainscoting, the moldings around the 9-foot windows, the transoms over the doors, and the trim in the rooms. The ceilings downstairs are 12 feet high, and those upstairs are not much lower. The feeling of the inn is quite Victorian, but as innkeeper Ruthmary Jordan is quick to point out, it is not a museum, and the furnishings are not limited to one period. One guest room is painted with a shutter-green enamel and has white woodwork and a red mantel over its working fireplace. The floor is red, and there is wicker furniture and an old-fashioned iron-and-brass bed. Each guest room has a phone. Guests use antique armoires in the rooms in lieu of closets. For a morning treat, leave your blinds open when you retire: Sunlight shining through the stained glass will brighten your day. Breakfast, which is set out in the old armoire in the upstairs hall, includes, in addition to typical Continental-breakfast items, such special treats as apple dumplings and poached pears.

The Pride House is painted a rich caramel color with white gingerbread trim. The side lawn is shaded by an old pecan tree. A front porch beckons guests with its antique rocking chairs and secluded old porch swing.

In addition to the rooms in the main house, there are four in a guest house called the Dependency, originally built for servants, which resembles a life-size dollhouse.

Accommodations: 8 rooms with private bath. *Pets and children:* Permitted in the Dependency only. *Driving Instructions:* From the junction with Highway 59 in Jefferson, take Highway 49 (Broadway) east 3 blocks.

WISE MANOR

312 Houston Street, Jefferson, TX 75657. 214-665-2386. *Innkeeper:* Katherine Ramsay Wise. Open all year.

Wise Manor is a gem of a Victorian home. Looking as if it has just stepped out of a fairy tale, the little two-story cottage is painted in salmon tones with crisp, white gingerbread trim. Surrounded by large pecan trees, it peers out from behind a wrought-iron fence in the older section of town. Innkeeper Katherine Wise has furnished the house with Victorian pieces from three generations of her family. The look of the place is fresh and clean, with ruffled curtains at the windows and marble-topped tables adorned with fresh seasonal flowers in the guest rooms. Antique white bedspreads and folded appliquéd quilts cover ornate walnut beds. A Continental breakfast is served, although Mrs. Wise will arrange for a plantation breakfast at the nearby Excelsior House if desired.

Accommodations: 3 rooms with private bath. *Pets:* Not permitted. *Driving Instructions:* From the junction of I-20 and U.S. 59 drive north through Marshall and continue 17 miles to Jefferson.

Llano, Texas

THE BADU HOUSE

601 Bessemer, Llano, TX 78643. 915-247-4304. *Innkeepers:* Kathy and Lance Moran. Open all year.

Llano is a ranching town in the Texas hill country. One of its earliest buildings was the First National Bank, built in Italian Renaissance style in 1891. In 1898 Professor Badu and his wife, Charlie Neal Badu, bought the bank and made it into their home. The Badu family lived there until the late 1970s. The sturdy structure was transformed over the next few years into a fanciful country inn. The restoration was done under the expert guidance of Ann Ruff, the Lone Star State's leading authority on Texas country inns, who sold the inn to the Morans in 1985.

The Badu House is listed in the National Register of Historic Places. Among its notable features are unusual shutters and bronze and brass hardware, all original to the building. Guest rooms, which have paneling brought from England, are furnished with a variety of antiques including family heirlooms. The baths all have claw-footed tubs, brass fixtures, pedestal sinks, and pull-chain commodes.

The bar and dining rooms downstairs are also decorated with antiques and early photographs of the Badu family and Llano. The Badu House's pride and joy, the bar, is covered by a rare mineral, llanite, which was discovered by Professor Badu and is found only in Llano County.

Lunch and dinner are served to the public, with such specialties as Mississippi corn-fed catfish and Texas steaks. The restaurant is open Tuesday through Saturday. The Morans also have a tree-shaded beer garden out behind the inn.

Accommodations: 7 rooms, 5 with private bath. *Pets and children:* Not permitted. *Driving Instructions:* The inn is at the intersection of Routes 71, 16, and 29.

Marshall, Texas

MEREDITH HOUSE
410 East Meredith Street, Marshall, TX 75670. 214-935-7147. *Innkeepers:* Michael and Sandra Cason. Open all year.

Marshall, Texas, is an historic town near Jefferson. The town's first bed-and-breakfast inn is a restored Victorian home built at the turn of the century. It was purchased by the Casons from the County Historical Society when it had to be moved to make way for a commercial property. Today the inn is on two acres, offering handmade quilts, colorful afghans, four-poster beds, old rockers on the front porch, and nostalgic clawfooted bathtubs. Breakfast features sausage and eggs and homemade biscuits.

Accommodations: 3 rooms with private bath. *Smoking:* Not permitted. *Driving Instructions:* Exit west off Route 59 onto Route 43 (Pinecrest Drive). Turn right on Garrett Street and left onto Meredith Street.

Navasota, Texas

THE CASTLE INN
1403 E. Washington, Navasota, TX 77868. 409-825-8051. *Innkeepers:* Helen and Tim Urquhart. Open all year.

The Castle is a Victorian fantasy that includes yellow brick walls, a copper-roofed tower, 14-foot-high medallioned ceilings, elaborate woodwork and parquet floors, and beveled and stained-glass windows. Built in 1893, it remained in one family until 1956 and escaped many so-called "improvements." The innkeepers, Tim and Helen Urquhart, have filled the rooms with a collection of Victorian antiques. The entrance door sparkles with 100 beveled panes of glass. The glow of a twenty-foot-high stained-glass window lights the landing of the heavily carved spindle staircase. Upstairs are the guest rooms and an authentically decorated sitting balcony where a Continental breakfast is served. The tower sitting room is a favorite spot. Guest rooms are furnished with marble-topped bureaus and washstands, Oriental rugs, and unusual beds. One room, for example, has a Louisiana plantation bed, and another, a walnut half-tester.

Accommodations: 4 rooms with private bath. *Pets:* Not permitted. *Children:* Under 14 not permitted. *Driving Instructions:* From Houston take Route 290 to Hempstead, then Route 6 to Navasota and Route 105 (Washington Avenue). From Bryan take Route 6 south to Route 105 and turn right.

New Braunfels, Texas

FAUST HOTEL

240 South Seguin Avenue, New Braunfels, TX 78130. 512-625-7791. *Innkeeper:* Rena Whitley. Open all year.

The Faust Hotel underwent extensive restoration in 1982. The brick and carved stonework of the exterior were cleaned, and the interior was polished, painted, and redecorated. The four-story hotel, built in 1929, is a fashionable dining and overnight stop in the very heart of historic New Braunfels, and it retains the glamour of fifty years ago. The old-fashioned fans are augmented by air-conditioning, and there is cable color television in each guest room. The ambience is that of the 1920s and 1930s.

Guest rooms are individually decorated with comfortable furnishings, heavy armoires, and candlestick telephones. Each has original furniture, fixtures, patterned carpets, pictures, and memorabilia. Every room has its original bathroom. The one suite has a sitting room with a bar and eighteenth-century furnishings, as well as a king-size bed.

Downstairs the lobby clock still ticks away on the wall. The lobby-lounge has its original elaborately tiled floor complementing the heavy antique couches and chairs.

The dining room re-creates the era with its green plants and the dark woods of the bentwood chairs. The public and guests are offered breakfasts, luncheons, and dinners by a staff that dresses in 1920s uniforms. Room service is available.

Accommodations: 61 rooms with private bath; 1 suite. *Pets:* Not permitted. *Driving Instructions:* New Braunfels is 35 miles northeast of San Antonio, off I-35 just north of the highway. The hotel is three blocks from the scenic Comal River and half a block from the town square.

PRINCE SOLMS INN

    295 East San Antonio Street, New Braunfels, TX 78130. 512-625-9169. *Innkeeper:* Ruth L. Wood. Open all year.

New Braunfels, founded in 1845 by a German prince, Carl Solms-Braunfels, retains much of its German heritage. People flock from all over to celebrate Wurtsfest — a week-long festival of Bavarian dancing and feasting in late October. A popular tourist attraction, this historic town has been called "The Sausage Capital of Texas," "The Antiquing Capital of Texas," and "The Beauty Spot of Texas."

In the heart of town is the Prince Solms Inn. Built in 1898, it has spent most of its existence welcoming guests. The handsome Victorian structure is a tribute to the craftsmanship of its German builders. In recent years, the inn has been restored and many antique fixtures and accessories have been added that enhance its period decor. Carriage lights flanking the tall entranceway came from a manor house in Texas; solid bronze doorknobs and hinges, from an aging Chicago mansion; and the ceiling fans with their antique lighting fixtures, from an early San Antonio building.

The Prince Solms's guest parlor and bedrooms are furnished with Victorian antiques. The inn exemplifies the area's historic past, and unobtrusive tours are offered to the public each afternoon. A few concessions have been made to modern-day comfort, including air conditioning and heating. The lone television set is hidden in an antique linen press in the parlor. A buffet breakfast is set out in the hall, and guests may take the food to their rooms, which contain breakfast areas.

The inn's restaurant and turn-of-the-century lounge-bar are in its basement, with 30-inch-thick stone walls and floor of polished brown concrete that appears to be made of leather. The restaurant, Wolfgang's Keller, features steaks, chicken, and veal specialties, accompanied by light sauces and brown rice.

One block from the inn is Landa Park and the crystal-clear spring-fed Comal River. Here, guests can bike, swim, golf, and enjoy boating in a scenic setting. At the nearby Guadalupe River, canoeing, rafting, and tubing are popular pastimes. River Road follows the Guadalupe beside its white-water rapids, cypress trees, and 200-foot-high cliffs. The river ends below the Canyon Lake Dam, an 8,000-acre lake.

Accommodations: 11 rooms with private bath. *Pets and children:* Not permitted. *Driving Instructions:* New Braunfels is just north of San Antonio, on I-35.

Rio Grande City, Texas

LA BORDE HOUSE

601 East Main Street, Rio Grande, TX 78582. 512-487-5101. *Innkeeper:* Jose M. Guerra. Open all year.

François La Borde commissioned Parisian architects to design his home, which is just a block from the Rio Grande River. Over the years, La Borde House acquired various additions and served for much of that time as a travelers' way station. Early guests included those traveling to Texas political events, riverboat travelers, and cattle barons who sold their herds on nearby river docks.

The hotel was purchased recently by the Sheerin family of San Antonio, who sponsored its restoration with the guidance of the Texas Historical Commission and the U.S. Department of the Interior. The thorough restoration included reconstructing all the inn's windows, recarving many of the wooden stair balusters, and hand-cutting many replacement pieces of gingerbread trim. The decorative iron gate was rebuilt to look as it did in 1898, giving the entrance to La Borde House a look reminiscent of New Orleans. The hotel is constructed largely of brick, and replacements were obtained from the same Carmargo, Mexico, brickyard where the original bricks were cast.

The hotel's furniture was collected throughout the South and West and is typical of the period, and there are Oriental rugs and English Axminster carpets throughout. Each bedroom bears a name commemorating a bit of local history. Many of the papers and fabrics are the same as those used during the recent restoration of the Texas Governor's Mansion. In one guest room a massive carved half-tester Victorian bed is cooled by the slowly turning blades of an illuminated ceiling fan. A caned rocker in another room sits beside a bed backed by an antique bookcase filled with century-old bound volumes. In a third room a high-back bed has 7-foot posts rising to a pleated full canopy. Along with the authentic rooms and their furnishings there are modern amenities, including full baths, many with pull-chain toilets, clawfooted bathtubs, pedestal sinks, and tile floors. Eight-channel television is available in all guest rooms and a wide selection of movies is available for showing in the parlor, with advance notice. Guests may relax in the parlor and library, as well as in a tropical courtyard.

Accommodations: 8 restored guest rooms with private bath, plus 13 one-room efficiency apartments. *Pets:* Not permitted. *Driving Instructions:* Take Route 83 to Rio Grande City.

San Marcos, Texas

CRYSTAL RIVER INN

326 West Hopkins, San Marcos, TX 78666. 512-396-3739. *Innkeepers:* Mike and Cathy Dillon. Open all year.

In Texas hill country, if you are lucky enough to be here in springtime, you can delight in rolling meadows of bluebonnets. Mike and Cathy Dillon's 100-year-old house, with imposing columns supporting two-story verandas, is the place to enjoy it from.

Crystal River Inn's guest rooms are each named for a Texas river, with color schemes and decor reflecting the feeling of each river. The Frio room is painted sky-blue and white and is furnished with wicker. The Medina room is white-on-white, with overstuffed furniture, antique satin fabrics, and mirrored tables. Pedernales is warm and casual, with country antiques and a canopied bed.

Breakfasts feature Cathy's home-baked pastries or her special beer biscuits with cheese and sausage on the side. In the library, the innkeepers join guests for evening get-togethers. There is a private lake nearby, and tubing and canoeing on the San Marcos River are popular activities. Mike and Cathy acquired a neighboring Victorian house and have transformed it into the inn's luxurious annex, adding three additional guestrooms.

Accommodations: 7 rooms, 5 with private bath. *Pets:* Not permitted. *Children:* Under 12 not permitted. *Driving Instructions:* From I-35 exit onto Route 205 west, which becomes Hopkins Street; the inn is 3 blocks past the courthouse.

Schulenburg, Texas

VON MINDEN HOTEL

607 Lyons Street, Schulenburg, TX 78956. 409-743-3493. *Innkeepers:* Bill and Betty Pettit. Open all year.

The Von Minden Hotel seems to exist in the 1930s or 1940s. Guests walking into the lobby would have no way of knowing they were in the second half of the twentieth century. Little has changed. Overstuffed chairs and couches are grouped together. Old radios are set on shelves, a dark wood-paneled phone booth stands next to the front desk, and a tiny antique shop is tucked into a corner by the stairs. Likewise, the guest rooms have changed little. If one wants to know what it was like to stay in an old salesman's hotel, this is it.

A half century ago it was a common practice for rural Texas hotels to also house a movie theater. Now the Von Minden's Cozy Theater is the last one of its kind in the state. As one walks down the second-floor hallway in the evening, the clicking of the ancient movie projector can be heard.

The guest rooms are furnished with sturdy mission-style furniture made by the men who built the hotel. The bathrooms have the original fixtures, including enameled tin tubs. The iron beds are set on braided rugs, and a Gideon Bible rests on each bedside table. Although the hotel is almost exactly as it was in earlier days, it is tidy and clean. With a bow to modern comfort, the rooms are air-conditioned (in case the paddle fans can't do the job), and color television sets have been installed. On the third floor, the Hard Times Restaurant and Bar offers steaks and seafood nightly to guests and the public.

Accommodations: 40 rooms, 20 with private bath. *Pets:* Not permitted. *Driving Instructions:* From I-10 take the Schulenburg exit south to the town. The inn is on Lyons Street, one block south of Main Street.

Weimar, Texas

WEIMAR COUNTRY INN
101 Jackson Street, Weimar, TX 78962. 409-725-8888. *Innkeeper:* Angela Teas. Open all year.

The town of Weimar was founded in the 1870s when railroad construction crossed the Colorado River and headed toward San Antonio. Among those who let the tracks cross their land were Mr. Borden, the inventor of canned milk, and Mr. Jackson, on whose land the railroad depot would be built and around which Weimar would grow.

The Jackson Hotel, built in 1875 to accommodate rail travelers, burned in 1900 and was rebuilt on the same spot. In 1981 the hotel was bought by a group of investors, restored, and renovated. Today it is a small inn furnished with country-Victorian antiques set off by polished floors and old-fashioned wallpapers. The dining room serves family-style meals Friday through Sunday, featuring house specialties such as Texas fried steaks, blackened snapper, and Mexican fried shrimp.

A Continental breakfast is set out in the sitting room upstairs. The guest rooms have stained-glass transoms, lace curtains, antiques, and hand-made quilts that reflect the soft colors of the floral wallpapers. The ceiling fans are supplemented by air-conditioning.

Accommodations: 9 rooms, 7 with private bath. *Pets:* Not permitted. *Driving Instructions:* Take Route 155 off I-10 and drive to Route 90. Turn left and go to the second light. Turn left again, and cross the tracks to Jackson and Center streets.

230 / VIRGINIA

Virginia

Abingdon, Virginia

The resort town of Abingdon, just above the Tennessee border in the Virginia Highlands, is the seat of Washington County and the center of Virginia's burley tobacco market. There is a *Burley Tobacco Festival* the first weekend of every October, and in the first two weeks of August, the county celebrates with the *Virginia Highlands Festival*. Tourists and native Virginians flock to Abingdon to hear the Highlands musical entertainments see plays, and browse among the rustic-crafts exhibits and demonstrations. The most famous attraction in town is the historic *Barter Theater*, across from the Martha Washington Inn on Main Street. The theater is now the State Theater of Virginia, performing a wide range of plays and offering a special children's theater as well. Performances run from April through October, and the children's show is from the middle of June through August. For information, call 703-628-3991.

THE MARTHA WASHINGTON INN

150 West Main Street, Abingdon, VA 24210. 703-628-3161. *Innkeeper*: Jim Watts. Open all year.

The Martha Washington Inn is a historic beauty that has recently been the object of a costly and comprehensive restoration, during which some 400 antiques were refurbished. The grounds were landscaped to provide a properly elegant setting. The interior, with its gracious broad hall and fine parlors, harbors many of the antiques originally in

the house. A particularly fine grandfather clock still keeps time from its station in the front lobby, shaded by a colonnaded veranda. Some of the most impressive furniture resides in the guest rooms, where guests may spend their nights under the high canopy of an elaborately carved bed in one room or in Victorian splendor in another. Some of the rooms have working fireplaces. Suites have modern bathrooms, complete with whirlpools and saunas.

The Martha Washington Inn began in 1832 as the private home of Patrick Henry's niece and her husband, General Francis Preston. In 1854 it became a Methodist women's college, which operated through the Civil War. The romance of this period has led to many stories concerning wounded soldiers and the college girls, secret staircases, floors with unremovable bloodstains, and phantom horses. The best known of these eerie tales concerns a mortally wounded Yankee soldier's being nursed by a Southern girl: She played her violin softly to him each evening to comfort him. His death broke her heart, and today some say one can still hear the strains of a ghostly violin around midnight on certain evenings.

First Lady's Table, the inn's restaurant, offers a selection of traditional Southern favorites, as well as Continental cuisine such as duckling with cognac, filet mignon stuffed with fresh oysters and wrapped with bacon, and poulet des pommes — boned chicken breast stuffed with apple and walnuts and topped with a light brandied cream sauce.

On warm, pleasant afternoons the old-fashioned rocking chairs on the inn's front porch are filled with guests taking the fresh air and enjoying the complimentary afternoon tea service. From May through October the historic Barter Theatre across the street (affiliated with the State Theatre of Virginia) offers a variety of plays for children or for adults.

Accommodations: 61 rooms and suites with private bath. *Pets:* Not permitted. *Driving Instructions:* Take exit 8 off I-81. The inn is in the heart of Abingdon.

Aldie, Virginia

LITTLE RIVER INN

U.S. 50, Aldie, Virginia. Mailing address: P.O. Box 116, Aldie, VA 22001. 703-327-6742. *Innkeeper:* Lee Tomassoni; owner: Tucker Withers. Open all year.

The Little River Inn is a country house of painted brick with wavy tiny-paned windows flanked by dark shutters. Evidence of the loving care this old house receives is in its trim border gardens, which skirt the veranda and back patio. Crisp ruffled curtains at the windows; pine, cherry, and walnut antique furnishings; and fires in the hearths add to the welcoming atmosphere.

Reconstructed in 1868 using the brick walls of an 1810 house, the building was completely restored in 1982, opening as an inn that same year. The guest rooms are decorated with antiques and early quilts. Some rooms have hand-stenciled borders, and one has a fireplace in its sitting area. In 1983, an adjacent log cabin and the eighteenth-century Patent House were also restored, as was the nearby Hill House. Each has a sitting room with a fireplace and wide-plank floors. A full complimentary breakfast is served here or in the main house. The Little River Inn is just 35 miles from Washington, D.C., in the heart of Virginia's hunt country. Middleburg and Leesburg are nearby, with shops, restaurants, and historic sites.

Accommodations: 5 rooms, 2 with private bath, and 3 cottages. *Pets:* Not permitted. *Children:* Under 10 not permitted. *Driving Instructions:* From Washington, D.C., drive west on I-66 to the U.S. 50 exit. Continue west on U.S. 50 for 16 miles.

Alexandria, Virginia

MORRISON HOUSE

116 South Alfred Street, Alexandria, Virginia. Mailing address: P.O. Box 19927, Alexandria, VA 22320. 703-838-8000 or 800-367-0800 (nationally) or 800-533-1808 (in Virginia). *Innkeepers:* Mr. and Mrs. Robert E. Morrison. Open all year.

In the heart of Alexandria's Old Town is this 47-room hotel that has the appearance of a manor house and the service of an intimate European auberge. It has been re-created by the Morrisons, who worked with designers and the Smithsonian Institution's building curator to assure the authenticity of the Federal style. The rooms are decorated with formal period antiques and artwork, as well as Baccarat crystal chandeliers and sconces set against a backdrop of Italian marble floors, mahogany paneling, and thick carpeting. There are burnished gold washbasins, marble baths, and a domed elevator with a *trompe l'oeil* sky and clouds. The guest rooms and suites have oversized mahogany beds and antique armoires. In the late afternoon, butlers serve a traditional English tea in the parlor. The restaurant, Le Chardon d'Or, serves nouvelle French cuisine.

Accommodations: 47 rooms with private bath. *Pets:* Not permitted. *Driving Instructions:* From Washington, D.C., turn off George Washington Parkway/Washington Street at King Street, going left. South Alfred Street will be the second street.

Charlottesville, Virginia

SILVER THATCH INN
3001 Hollymead Drive, Charlottesville, VA 22901. 804-978-4686.
Innkeepers: Tim and Shelley Dwight. Open all year except Christmas and the first two weeks in January.

Silver Thatch Inn is a Colonial building with a long and interesting history. The first section was built in 1780 by Hessian soldiers captured at the Battle of Saratoga in New York, who were marched to Charlottesville and instructed to build their own barracks. In 1801 the building was enlarged and converted to a boys' school. Later it saw service as a tavern and coach stop and, still later, as a private plantation. In the 1930s, with another addition, it became the home of a dean at the University of Virginia.

Tim and Shelley Dwight purchased the sprawling white clapboard building in 1984 and have since transformed it into an attractive inn, once again offering food and lodging to travelers. The inn is furnished with antique beds, dressers, and armoires accented by country-style quilts. With a bow to modern amenities, there are tennis courts and a swimming pool on the landscaped grounds. The three "country formal" dining rooms feature French cuisine served by candlelight. Five entrées are prepared nightly by chef-innkeeper Shelley Dwight.

Accommodations: 8 rooms with private bath. *Pets:* Not permitted.
Driving Instructions: From Charlottesville, take Route 29 north 8 miles to the inn.

Chincoteague, Virginia

THE CHANNEL BASS INN

100 Church Street, Chincoteague, VA 23336. 804-336-6148. *Innkeeper*: James S. Hanretta. Open all year except Christmas and New Years day; restaurant closed Monday.

The exterior of the Channel Bass Inn gives no real hint of the pleasures awaiting inside its doors. This island house grew up as the need arose after it was built in the 1860s. Over the years, a third floor with lots of dormers was added, as well as a glassed-in porch complete with such modern touches as asbestos shingle on the walls and asphalt shingle on the roof. But guests who venture inside will find a unique gastronomic experience.

Jim Hanretta, the owner-chef, trained in Spain and France. Dinners here reflect Jim's respect for food, his affection for Spanish culture and the Basque countryside, and his reliance on the sea's bountiful provisions. Five choices of seafood appetizers include oysters Basque (with parmesan cheese, chorizo sausage, and tomato sauce), oysters continental (in a tarragon wine sauce), and steamed Chincoteague clams. Specialties included in eleven entrées are crab soufflé for two prepared at the table, and trois de mer (shrimp, scallops, and lobster sautéed in white wine, butter, and garlic). There are also additional seafood dishes, beef dishes, and a special rice dish that is an aromatic blend of saffron, rice, pepper, onion, tomato, chicken stock, and chorizo sausage. Prices at the Channel Bass are higher than at many Southern inns.

The inn's guest rooms vary in both size and furnishings. The third floor has been restored, and the second floor is mostly original. All rooms are furnished simply, some with antiques, others with reproductions. Two furnished suites have the added luxury of room service.

The innkeeper offers cooking seminars in the off season: Rates over three days include lodging, meals, and three four-hour seminars.

Accommodations: 10 rooms with private bath. *Pets:* Not permitted. *Children:* Under 11 not permitted. *Driving Instructions:* From Salisbury, Maryland, take Route 13 south approximately 40 miles to Route 175, and then to Chincoteague. When Route 175 becomes a dead end on Main Street, turn left, go two blocks to Church Street, and turn right. The inn is the first house on the right.

MISS MOLLY'S INN

113 North Main Street, Chincoteague, VA 23336. 804-336-6686. *Innkeepers:* Dr. and Mrs. James C. Stam. Open April through November.

Chincoteague is an unspoiled island, famous for its wild ponies, oysters, and clam shoals. The windswept beauty of nearby Assateague National Seashore and Chincoteague National Wildlife Refuge are minutes away. This inn, an ideal base for enjoying all that the islands and little fishing village have to offer, is a large Queen Anne–style Victorian just 150 feet from the shore and docking oyster boats. It was built in 1886 by Mr. Rowley. His daughter Molly lived in the house for eighty-four years and was one of the island's best-loved citizens. How could the inn be called anything but Miss Molly's?

Four porches offer views of spectacular sunsets over the water, and there are gazebos and picket fences set off by pink and red roses. The 25-room house is furnished with antiques and is completely air conditioned. A portrait of Miss Molly hangs in the stairwell. The innkeepers, Jim and Priscilla, restored the inn, papering the rooms with flowered and striped wallpapers and putting lace curtains on the windows. The Stams serve a full breakfast and afternoon tea to overnight guests.

Accommodations: 7 rooms, 1 with private bath. *Pets:* Not permitted. *Children:* Under twelve not permitted. *Driving Instructions:* From Salisbury, Maryland, take Route 13 south to Route 175 and then drive eastward. At Chincoteague Island, turn left on Main Street and drive 2½ blocks to the inn.

Fredericksburg, Virginia

RICHARD JOHNSTON INN

711 Caroline Street, Fredericksburg, VA 22401. 703-899-7606. *Innkeeper:* Libby Gowin. Open all year.

Fredericksburg has a large historic district that includes George Washington's mother's home, James Monroe's law office, the Rising Sun Tavern, and Civil War battlefields. The Richard Johnston Inn, a Federal-style inn built in 1789, is in the historic Old Town. The common rooms—a sitting room, the library, and a banquet-style dining room—are furnished with formal Colonial antiques. Guest rooms are furnished with Early American and English antiques, although the suites have period reproduction pieces. All the rooms have floral country-style wallpapers and handmade quilts on the beds; seven rooms have working fireplaces. Breakfast is served on the brick patio by the river or by the fireside.

Accommodations: 11 rooms, 7 with private bath. *Driving Instructions:* The inn is in downtown Fredericksburg, across the street from the Visitors' Center.

Hamilton, Virginia

HAMILTON GARDEN INN
353 West Colonial Highway, Hamilton, VA 22068. 703-338-3693 or 338-2033. *Innkeepers:* Bill and Lucinda Mitchell. Open all year. Restaurant closed Tuesdays.

Hamilton Garden Inn is an 1868 summer estate ideally located in Northern Virginia's Hunt Country, not far from the nation's capital. The inn, with its restaurant, is a new venture for chef-innkeepers Bill and Lucinda Mitchell. They chose bright colors for the inn, hung lace curtains, and furnished the rooms with Victorian antiques. A library and parlor adjoin two dining rooms, where contemporary American cuisine is served, including fresh seafood from the Chesapeake Bay and locally raised beef, lamb, and pork.

Guest rooms, decorated in Victorian motifs, have handmade quilts or crocheted spreads on antique beds. In addition to the public rooms downstairs, there is a small wicker-furnished sitting room upstairs where guests may relax. Outside, the deck leads to an English-style garden with cobblestone walks.

Accommodations: 3 rooms with shared bath. *Pets:* Not permitted. *Driving Instructions:* Take Route 7 six miles west of Leesburg to Route 704, go south 1/4 mile to Colonial Highway and turn right.

Hot Springs, Virginia

THE HOMESTEAD

Route 220, Hot Springs, VA 24445. 703-839-5500. Open all year. More than three centuries ago, an American Indian brave discovered warm mineral water bubbling out of a fissure in the earth. Almost without a pause since the mid-seventeenth century, guests seeking the healthful waters have been drawn to the towns of Hot Springs and Warm Springs. The Homestead in Hot Springs is a very special Southern resort that has offered an unbroken tradition of pampering its guests with almost any imaginable service and fine food since the first hotel was built on its grounds in 1891. The tone of our visit was established the moment we stepped through the Homestead's doors into its Great Hall. The strains of a string ensemble playing for guests at teatime greeted us, and we were instantly transported to another era.

This is no quaint little inn. There seem to be miles of corridors at The Homestead. Its guest rooms and parlors accommodate 1,000 guests, and the staff in attendance always exceeds the number of people registered. Guests may choose between a recently constructed ultramodern hotel wing and the more traditional rooms in the earlier section that we prefer. There, the decor and furnishings are reminiscent of a fine European hotel, and the service blends European traditions with Southern hospitality. The arrangement of much of The Homestead is of bedrooms separated by parlor rooms. Thus there is the choice of renting one room, or several suite combinations. For the kind of splurge that the Homestead is likely to be, we recommend adding the small charge for a parlor room.

Included in the daily rate at the Homestead are the rooms, two full meals, use of the indoor pool, a nightly movie, dancing, and afternoon tea. For additional charges one may enjoy bowling, carriage rides, golfing on three eighteen-hole courses, ice-skating, skiing on the Homestead slopes within walking distance of the hotel, tennis, and spa facilities including mineral baths, massage, steam room, and sauna.

For us, all of these recreational facilities took a backseat to what must be described as the Homestead's awesome parade of food from dawn to dusk. We stopped trying to count the hot and cold dishes on the breakfast buffet, but have it on good authority that the luncheon offerings usually reach 150 items. At dinner an elegant à la carte menu, different each day, offers up to a dozen special entrées. The Continental cuisine offered at the Homestead is prepared by a staff of sixty-five cooks, bakers, and pastry men and served in the dining room by a veritable army of highly trained waiters. The Homestead's traditions date back more than a century; it is certainly a very special place.

Accommodations: 600 rooms. *Driving Instructions:* Ask for the Homestead's brochure detailing the best routes.

VINE COTTAGE INN

Route 220, Hot Springs, Virginia. Mailing address: P.O. Box 918, Hot Springs, VA 24445. 703-839-2422. *Innkeepers:* Wendell and Pat Lucas. Open all year.

The Vine Cottage Inn is just 500 yards from the famed "country spa" the Homestead, in the Warm Springs Mountains of the Alleghenies. The cottage was built in 1903 as an annex to the historic hotel by its owners, the Virginia Hot Springs Inc. The inn's wide veranda is lined with white-wicker rockers. Flowers, shrubbery, and the forested mountains are the backdrop for the big turn-of-the-century house with its many-angled gables and wraparound porch. Pat and Wendell keep busy restoring, refinishing, and adding to their eclectic collection of antiques. Two of the guest rooms are dorms that sleep up to six people each and are popular with hunting, fishing, and skiing groups and with large families. The other guest rooms have the old-fashioned look and feel of the early 1900s. There is a sink in each room, and eight of the rooms have private baths with claw-footed tubs. Other individual baths are down the hall, as they were in Grandma's day. Many of the beds are covered with the original "Vine Cottage" embroidered spreads.

The inn's spacious living room invites guests to relax and chat with fellow lodgers or to curl up by the fire with a book from the walnut bookcases.

The Vine Cottage Inn is popular in all four seasons, with cross-country and downhill skiing at the Homestead nearby, trout fishing in national-forest brooks in the spring, hiking in the summer, and spectacular foliage and hunting every autumn. A complimentary breakfast is served.

Accommodations: 14 rooms, 8 with private bath. *Driving Instructions:* The inn is next to the Homestead on Route 220, within the town limits of Hot Springs, 5 miles south of Warm Springs.

Howardsville, Virginia

FISH POND PLANTATION
Route 1, Box 48, Howardsville, VA 24562. 804-263-4484. *Innkeeper:* Al Byrne. Open all year.

This 1840 slate-roofed country estate is part of 1,215 acres of rolling meadows, forest trails, and river frontage in the Blue Ridge foothills of central Virginia. Sycamores and oaks surround the plantation house and its dependencies—an icehouse, smokehouse, pheasant and quail houses, and former slave quarters. One cottage has been transformed into a guest hideaway. The other guest rooms are in the main house, with its nooks and crannies and sloping eaves.

Full breakfasts are served in the dining room or on the patio. Lunch or dinner can be arranged with three days' advance reservations. Recreational activities include guided canoe, raft, and tubing trips, fishing on the James River, hunting (in season), and hiking on the inn's trails.

Accommodations: 7 rooms, 5 with private bath. *Driving Instructions:* Take Route 6 to Route 626 and turn west. Drive 2.1 miles past Howardsville to a gravel drive and the signs "Highland on the James" and "Fish Pond Plantation." Turn left and follow the signs.

Lancaster, Virginia

THE INN AT LEVELFIELDS
Route 3, Lancaster, Virginia. Mailing address: P.O. Box 216, Lancaster, VA 22503. 804-435-6887. *Innkeepers:* Doris and Warren Sadler. Open all year.

This Southern mansion, built in 1857, is a hip-roofed Georgian-style Colonial. It was one of the last antebellum plantations built in the commonwealth. A thousand-foot drive flanked by meadows and a brick walk lined with towering English boxwoods are the approach to this inn set on 54 acres of forest, lawn, and gardens.

The Sadlers have restored the inn and furnished it with family heirlooms, period antiques, and Oriental carpets. Two formal dining rooms offer candlelit dining to overnight guests and the public (Wednesdays through Saturdays), as well as a Sunday brunch. Lunch and dinner feature fresh seasonal seafood from the Chesapeake Bay. A complimentary breakfast is served to guests in the dining room or in their rooms. Guests may tour the many nearby historic sites, relax by the pool out back, or stroll the grounds.

Accommodations: 4 rooms with private bath. *Pets:* Not permitted. *Driving Instructions:* From Kilmarnock, Virginia, take Route 3 west to the inn.

Leesburg, Virginia

LAUREL BRIGADE INN

20 West Market Street, Leesburg, VA 22075. 703-777-1010. *Innkeeper*: Ellen Flippo Wall. Open mid-February through December.

The Laurel Brigade Inn is a handsome 1759 structure of cut-and-fitted native Virginia stone. Its entranceway is framed by a rare ivy that spreads up one corner and across the lobby's side porch. The innkeeper, Ellen Wall, is constantly asked for cuttings. Guests enter the inn through the lobby, which doubles as a sitting room and is furnished with antiques and appropriate reproductions. There are delicate "lady's chairs," a Chippendale sofa, and an enormous table of rare black Italian marble that many visitors say is quite valuable and that Ellen claims was left by the previous owners because it was too heavy to move. Five guest rooms with spacious private baths are available to overnight guests. Each is decorated with quilt-covered canopied bedsteads and a combination of period antiques and suitable reproductions, which are handcrafted by Clore, a group of fifth-generation German cabinetmakers who fashion pieces without using glue or nails.

The Laurel Brigade's meals attract hungry Washingtonians to Leesburg. The dining rooms vary in size and atmosphere from the hundred-seat main dining room, which opens through French doors onto enclosed gardens, to snug cubbyholes. Meals feature simple, plentiful dishes at reasonable prices. House specialties include such fresh seafood dishes as Laurel crab cakes and flounder stuffed with crabmeat, and country-fried chicken, Virginia ham, and steaks. Three fresh vegetables are passed family-style at the evening meals and Sundays, and there are baskets of hot rolls on the tables. The inn is famous for its home-baked pastries, and in a vote on favorites, apple pie would probably win hands down. The restaurant is open from noon to 2 for lunch and 5 to 8 for dinner. Sunday meals run from noon to 7, and the restaurant is closed Monday.

Accommodations: 5 rooms with private bath. *Driving Instructions:* Leesburg is on Route 7, and the inn is in the center of town, half a block west off U.S. 15.

THE NORRIS HOUSE INN

108 Loudoun Street, S.W., Leesburg, Virginia. Mailing address: P.O. Box 966, Leesburg, VA 22075. 703-777-1806. *Innkeepers:* Amy and Craig DeRemer and Holly Stanley. Open all year.

The Norris House Inn was built in 1806 on a narrow side street in historic Leesburg, just one hour from Washington, D.C. A worn brick sidewalk runs past the inn's brick-enclosed side yard, with its tall pines, magnolia tree, flower gardens, and decorative antique sleigh. In warm weather red geraniums add bright color to the orange brick building, with its dark green shutters and sturdy double front door.

Just above this entryway a glassed-in sitting room juts out. Downstairs there is an inviting parlor on either side of the hall. The original interior shutters are still at all the windows, which have old wavy glass in their tiny twelve-over-twelve panes. One of the two parlors is decorated in blues and whites, with a blue-and-white sofa facing an ornate fireplace and an old-fashioned Victrola standing in the corner. The other contains formal Victorian pieces, including an oak settee and an antique parlor organ. Old oil paintings add to its appeal. Local craftsmen frequently display their work in the public rooms. The dining room's trim is accented in Victorian fashion with cinnamon and coffee colors above walnut wainscoting. A large pewter chandelier lights the polished antique table, with its bouquet of fresh flowers. A built-in walnut hutch holds a silver tea service. It is here that breakfast is served. The morning meal usually includes several specialties, such as lemon muffins, fried apples, or salmon quiche.

Each guest room is furnished with antiques, and two have working fireplaces. Antique quilts, many from the families of the innkeepers, top guest room beds, including a queen-size four-poster in one room and a canopied bed in another. Personal touches at Norris House include complimentary port and sherry in the evening and chocolates made especially for the inn, which are left on guests' pillows at night.

The Norris House Inn is in Virginia's hunt country and is within easy access to many antique shops and restaurants.

Accommodations: 6 rooms with 3 shared baths. *Pets:* Not permitted. *Children:* Young children not encouraged. *Driving Instructions:* From Washington, D.C., take Route 7 into Leesburg. Keep left at the fork and then drive four blocks to the inn, which will be on your right.

Lexington, Virginia

HISTORIC COUNTRY INNS OF LEXINGTON
11 Main Street, Lexington, VA 24450. 703-463-2044. *Innkeeper:* Don Fredenburg. Open all year.

Three buildings of historic significance comprise the Historic Country Inns of Lexington, each owned and restored by the Peter Meredith family and managed by Don Fredenburg. The Alexander-Winthrow House and McCampbell Inn are on Main Street opposite each other in the center of town, with their reception desk at McCampbell Inn. Alexander-Winthrow House, built in 1789 of patterned, glazed bricks, has a lower stone section housing a bookshop, and in the past served as Lexington's first school, first post office, and first bank. Today it offers several floors of guest suites. The McCampbell Inn, built as a townhouse in 1809—two wings were added during the ensuing fifty years—is decorated with eighteenth- and nineteenth-century antiques. Its fourteen guest rooms and two suites have refreshment bars stocked with coffee, tea, and juice. Breakfast is served in its Great Room downstairs.

Maple Hall, the Merediths' latest acquisition, is an 1850 plantation house on fifty-six pastoral acres, six miles north of the city. Its thirteen guest rooms, also decorated with antiques, all have working fireplaces.

Breakfast is served in the dining room, and guests may, by advance reservation, have dinner.

Accommodations: 36 rooms and suites with private bath. *Driving Instructions:* Take I-81 to the Lexington exit. McCampbell Inn (main desk) is at the corner of Main and Washington streets. Inquire for full directions to Maple Hall.

Mathews, Virginia

RIVERFRONT HOUSE

Route 14 East, Mathews, Virginia. Mailing address: P.O. Box 310, Mathews, VA 23109. 804-725-9975. *Innkeeper:* Annette Waldman Goldreyer. Open mid-April to mid-November.

Years ago, daffodils were a major crop in this town, and they still spring up wild each April. Riverfront House, with its own dock for crabbing and boating, is on seven acres at the edge of Put In Creek, near the mouth of the East River. This 1840 farmhouse, with its wrap-around veranda, is less than an hour from Williamsburg and Busch Gardens.

Inside, the inn has a gracious entrance hall and staircase, mahogany mantels in the living room, and lace curtains throughout. Colorful scatter rugs decorate the air-conditioned bedrooms. A breakfast of fresh fruits, cheeses, breads, and muffins is served in the dining room or, in good weather, outdoors, if guests prefer.

Mathews is a sleepy village which dates from Revolutionary times. There are craft shops and restaurants in town within walking distance of the inn. Chesapeake Bay is nearby, and two riverfront seafood restaurants are within five miles.

Accommodations: 7 rooms, 3 with private bath. *Pets:* Not permitted. *Driving Instructions:* Take Route 17 south through Saluda to Glenns, then Route 198 to Route 14 East into Mathews and continue east for 9/10 mile. The inn is the third driveway past the bus shelter, on the right.

Middleburg, Virginia

Middleburg is in the heart of Virginia's hunt country with rolling hills and country fields neatly bounded by age-old fieldstone walls. It is an area of great beauty and half-hidden horse farms and estates. The picture-postcard town is only 25 miles from Dulles Airport and 50 miles from the nation's capital. Middleburg consists of historic old brick and native-stone buildings housing little shops and eateries. The *Middleburg Antiques Center*, one block west of the Red Fox Inn, is in a three-story restored old home. Here, twenty antiques dealers sell a wide range of pieces.

THE RED FOX INN & MOSBY'S TAVERN

East Washington Street, Middleburg, VA 22117. 703-687-6301 or 800-223-1728. *Innkeepers:* Turner and Dana Reuter. Open all year.

The Red Fox Inn, everything an eighteenth-century inn should be, got off to an auspicious start. In 1731, the land was surveyed by a lad of only sixteen—George Washington. A tavern had been located on the spot for three years, so the future president probably paused for refreshment before continuing his task. In time, the tavern came to be called Chinn's Ordinary, and by 1812, it had grown to thirty-five rooms with an extensive wine cellar. Called The Beveridge House for the next sixty-five years, the inn provided a meeting place for the Confederate General J. E. B. Stuart. In the midst of fierce fighting, he and Colonel John Mosby met there to plan their offensives, and a room today bears Mosby's name.

The 30-inch stone walls of the Red Fox Inn remain unscathed by time. After it was bought by Nancy Reuter in 1976, it received an exacting restoration. Extensive work was done to duplicate period wallpapers and to choose paint colors appropriate to the inn's eighteenth-century heritage. Each of the inn's many mantels (ten of the fireplaces are in guest rooms) were carefully stripped of layers of paint and redone. Each mantel is different; the one in the Mosby room is particularly distinctive, with a tall, six-paneled front. The guest-room fireplaces and those in the public rooms are in full working order.

The main dining room (one of seven) is characterized by heavy, 16-inch-square posts that are hung with copper pots and support the dark-beamed ceiling. Windsor chairs, tavern tables, and hunt memorabilia set the mood. Country breakfasts, lunches, and candlelight dinners are available to guests and the public. The wine list includes selections from nearby vineyards. Mosby's Tavern is the inn's pub and more casual restaurant with oak paneling and stenciled ceilings. A champagne brunch is served Saturdays and Sundays.

The Red Fox Inn's guest rooms are decorated and furnished with antiques. Most of the four-poster beds have canopies, and several rooms have their original fireplaces. Fresh flowers, bedside sweets, private phones, and thick cotton robes are thoughtful extra touches. Continental breakfast is served in the guest's rooms. The inn's complex includes the Stray Fox Inn, built before the Civil War. It has stenciled floors and walls, hooked rugs, and period antiques. Another in the complex is the nineteenth-century McConnell House, formerly the home of an early country doctor, and once known as The Pill Box.

Accommodations: 12 rooms with private bath. *Pets:* Not permitted. *Driving Instructions:* Take I-66 to Route 50, which leads directly to Middleburg and the inn.

WELBOURNE

Route 743, Middleburg, VA 22117. 703-687-3201. *Innkeeper:* Mrs. N. H. Morison. Open all year.

For almost a century and a half, Middleburg has been the undisputed center of fox hunting in America. The local hunt was founded in 1840 by Colonel Dulany, who also founded the country's oldest horse show, the Upperville Colt and Horse Show. Colonel Dulany lived in the family mansion known as Welbourne and was the great-grandfather of the current innkeeper's husband. In all, seven generations of the same family have occupied this superb old Virginia home; now, each year, privileged travelers may also stay here.

Welbourne was built in sections, beginning with a stone house constructed in 1775, with additions from 1820 through 1870. The mansion retains seven generations of family heirlooms in an especially Southern and refined atmosphere. Welbourne continues to be a working farm, and its rural location assures a tranquil stay. Five of the inn's guest rooms have working fireplaces, although a modest fee is charged for the firewood. In addition to the rooms within the mansion, there are two cottages on the grounds, each of which can sleep four. Each morning, guests are treated to a hearty Southern breakfast of sausage, grits, eggs, fried tomatoes or apples, and so on, served at the mansion's dining-room table.

One must assume that these meals are considerably more relaxed than the one enjoyed by General Jeb Stuart, who, it is reported, ate his morning meal at Welbourne on horseback in front of the porch as bullets ticked off the building's tin roof. In the 1920s, Scribner's editor Maxwell Perkins was a frequent visitor and often sent his more promising authors to Middleburg for relaxation. Thomas Wolfe and F. Scott Fitzgerald were among the prominent guests. Fitzgerald wrote that he was "fascinated with the quality of that place."

Accommodations: 7 rooms with private bath, plus 4 cottages.
Driving Instructions: From the center of Middleburg, take Route 50 3½ miles west to Route 611; turn right and go 1½ miles to Route 743. Turn left and drive 1.2 miles to the inn, on your left.

Monterey, Virginia

HIGHLAND INN

Main Street, Monterey, Virginia. Mailing address: P.O. Box 40, Monterey, VA 24465. 703-468-2143. *Innkeepers:* John and Eleanor Hulser. Open March through October.

The restoration of this historic old mountain resort, once known as the Monterey Hotel, won back its former reputation as "The Pride of the Mountains" and earned it a place in the National Register of Historic Places.

The Highland Inn, built in 1904, is a white clapboard structure dominating the main street of this hamlet. Two stories of gingerbreaded porches stretch across its facade. Some of the hotel's original iron bedsteads are still in use and Victorian and Edwardian antiques decorate the rooms. Colorful quilts brighten the beds, and country curtains decorate the windows. Halls are softly lighted by brass lamps with green glass shades. The ground floor's small, airy dining room serves three meals a day, with specialties of local trout and Virginia ham. On Sundays, the only meal served is a buffet brunch. The Black Sheep Tavern was recently added to the back of the hotel. The inn's old-fashioned parlor, with its fireplace, is a popular gathering spot for guests. The Highland Inn is in a historic district surrounded by more than 3 million acres of national forest.

Accommodations: 17 rooms with private bath. *Driving Instructions:* From Staunton, Virginia, take Route 250 west for 45 miles.

Mount Holly, Virginia

MOUNT HOLLY HOUSE

Route 202, Mount Holly, Virginia. Mailing address: P.O. Box 130, Mount Holly, VA 22524. 804-472-3336. *Innkeepers:* Bob Stolman and Rick Hall. Open all year.

Mount Holly House began in the mid-nineteenth century as a hotel for travelers on the steamboats that, until 1938, plied the rivers joining Washington and the tidewater towns of southern Virginia. One boat, the James Adams, was a floating theater that often docked at Mount Holly House and put on shows. Edna Ferber, author of Showboat, was a frequent traveler on this steamboat and a regular guest at the hotel.

Innkeepers Bob Stolman and Rick Hall have restored the inn to its Victorian best, filling its rooms with antiques and reproductions. Oriental rugs, four-poster beds with quilt coverings, and *objets d'art* grace the rooms, which overlook the river and the grounds. Breakfast and formal high tea are served daily, and guests are treated to bedtime brandy and mints. Dinner is available with advance notice.

Singalongs are popular, and occasionally an innkeeper can be persuaded to entertain at the 1831 square grand piano in the parlor. The hotel is on a small working farm with goats, chickens, and ducks. The river offers swimming, fishing, and crabbing, and a small sailboat is available. Bicycle tours introduce guests to Virginia's historic Northern Neck, encompassing vineyards, George Washington's birthplace, and Stratford Hall, home of Robert E. Lee. Three-day mid-week packages include an old-fashioned riverfront crab feast.

Accommodations: 14 rooms with shared baths. *Pets:* Not permitted. *Driving Instructions:* From Fredericksburg on Route 3, go three miles east of Montross; turn left on Route 202 and drive four miles to the Nomini bridge. Just after the bridge, turn left onto the first gravel road and drive 1/10 mile.

Nellysford, Virginia

TRILLIUM HOUSE

Wintergreen, Route 664, Nellysford, Virginia. Mailing address: P.O. Box 280, Nellysford VA 22958. 804-325-9126. *Innkeepers:* Ed and Betty Dinwiddie. Open all year.

The brainchild of Ed and Betty Dinwiddie, who decided that the only way to get everything they wanted in a country inn was to design it themselves, Trillium House combines the best of several worlds. An inn with an old-fashioned "curl-up-by-the-hearth-with-a-good-book" atmosphere, it is actually of recent construction (1982), with a host of modern amenities. Built almost entirely of cedar, the inn is alive with all the activities of a private mountain resort. It is surrounded by the Wintergreen Club and Resort, within easy reach of skiing, tennis, all-weather swimming, a health club, stables, and Devil's Knob Golf Course. Wintergreen's 10,000 acres also offer hiking, canoeing, and fishing.

The focal point of the inn is the Great Room, with its twenty-two-foot-high, exposed-beam ceiling and wood-burning stove. A balcony that houses a library is a wonderful spot to relax and gaze out of an arched floor-to-ceiling window. The inn's dining room, which overlooks a busy bird-feeding station, serves breakfasts and single-entrée dinners to guests and the public by reservation only. Carpeted guest rooms have painted walls displaying carefully selected works of art and a simplicity that gives prominence to the antiques and handsome quilts.

Accommodations: 12 rooms with private bath. *Pets:* Not permitted. *Driving Instructions:* From the Blue Ridge Parkway or Route 151, take Route 664 to Wintergreen Club and Resort and the inn.

Orange, Virginia

MAYHURST INN

Route 15 South, Orange, Virginia. Mailing address: P.O. Box 707, Orange, VA 22960. 703-672-5597. *Innkeepers:* Stephen and Shirley Ramsey. Open all year.

The Mayhurst Inn is a fanciful Italianate Victorian mansion on 36 acres of magnolias, towering oaks, and Osage orange trees, overlooking meadows with grazing cows, a farm pond, and the distant town of Orange. The mansion was built in 1859 by Colonel John Willis, great-nephew of President James Madison. Willis reportedly bought the land from Dolly Madison to help relieve her financial burdens. The house is now listed in the National Register of Historic Places.

Inside, a magnificent oval staircase ascends four floors to a rooftop gazebo. The Ramseys have furnished the rooms with a large collection of antiques, the overflow being offered for sale in their antique shop in the barn. Guest rooms, many with Palladian windows, balconies, and wallpaper, have wonderful beds, some high enough to require steps. A ground-floor guest room has its own patio, and both the room and patio are decorated with mountain twig furniture. There are three sitting rooms. Breakfast and afternoon tea are served in the dining room.

Accommodations: 7 rooms, 6 with private bath. *Driving Instructions:* From Charlottesville, take I-64 to Zions Crossroads and then follow Route 15 north. The inn is ¼ mile south of Orange on Rt. 15.

Paris, Virginia

ASHBY INN

Routes 759 and 701, Paris, Virginia. Mailing address: Route 1, Box 2A, Paris, VA 22130. 703-592-3900. *Innkeepers:* John and Roma Sherman. Open all year except two weeks in summer.

Paris, Virginia, is a tiny hamlet amid green, high mountain meadows and historic country houses. Ashby Inn, built in 1829, has tidy gardens and black shutters set against white stucco. The front dining room, the taproom, and the library all have working fireplaces, as does one guest room. The Shermans offer meals, prepared from fresh local ingredients, in the dining room or out on the patio. All rooms are furnished with early-nineteenth-century antiques and have sloping eaves, dormers, painted floors, rag rugs, and scenic views of the countryside from low, multipaned windows.

Accommodations: 6 rooms, 4 with private bath. *Pets:* Not permitted. *Children:* Under 10 not permitted. *Driving Instructions:* From Winchester, Virginia, take Route 50 east approximately 18 miles, cross over Ashby Gap, and take the first right at the bottom of the hill onto Route 759. The inn is at the east end of the village.

Richmond, Virginia

THE CATLIN-ABBOTT HOUSE

2304 East Broad Street, Richmond, VA 23223. 804-780-3746. *Innkeeper:* Frances L. Abbott. Open all year.

The Catlin-Abbott House was built in 1845, its superb brick masonry the mark of master craftsman William Mitchell, who was William Catlin's slave. So skilled was Mitchell that Catlin frequently hired him out to other Richmond families to build their homes. Mitchell's daughter, Maggie Walker, grew up to become this country's first woman bank president.

Everywhere one looks, the dignity of a fine Southern home is evident: Oriental rugs, Czechoslovakian crystal chandeliers, lace-trimmed four-poster beds, working fireplaces in most guest rooms, mahogany tables and chairs, and polished pine floors. From the inn's veranda, one can look out over the garden, which blooms almost continuously from March through November. In the morning, one may choose to have breakfast in bed or in the dining room, served on Lenox china, with sterling silver flatware. After breakfast, most guests make their first sightseeing stop at St. John's church, just a block away. It was here that Patrick Henry uttered the words, "Give me liberty or give me death."

Accommodations: 4 rooms, 3 with private bath, and a 2-bedroom suite. *Pets and children:* Not permitted. *Driving Instructions:* From I-95 northbound, take Exit 10 to the first traffic light (Broad Street), turn left and proceed east to the 2300 block.

Smith Mountain Lake, Virginia

HOLLAND-DUNCAN HOUSE
Routes 122 and 616, Smith Mountain Lake, Virginia. Mailing address: Route 3, Box 681, Moneta, VA 24121. 703-721-8510. *Innkeepers:* Kathryn and Clint Shay. Open all year.

This Federal-style house was built in 1820 from bricks made on the property. The front section of the inn has its original pine flooring and six fireplaces, several in the guest rooms. A formal dining room and Victorian-style sitting room are furnished with antiques. Boxwoods and climbing roses planted in the 1800s still flourish, while a former Confederate post office now serves as the Shays' office.

One guest room occupies the original kitchen—the old hearth and mantle are still used. Kathryn and Clint have also rebuilt the old log summer kitchen off the main house, salvaging a 7-foot hearth. The inn is close to Smith Mountain Lake and the birthplace of Booker T. Washington. Guests plan the day's outings over the Shay's "gourmet" breakfast.

Accommodations: 4 rooms, 2 with private bath. *Driving Instructions:* The inn is at the intersection of Routes 122 and 616.

Sperryville, Virginia

THE CONYERS HOUSE
Slate Mills Road, Sperryville, VA 22740. 703-987-8025. *Innkeepers:* Norman and Sandra Cartwright-Brown. Open all year.

The Conyers House is located, according to one of the local folks, "right there on Kilby's Creek at the foot of Walden Mountain by that ol' cottonwood tree. If you go by Dick Jenkin's white chickens, you done gone too far." After beginning as a store around 1770, acquiring an addition in 1810, and passing almost 200 years as, in turn, a tollhouse, post office, and country store, the rambling, four-story frame building was restored in 1979 and transformed into an appealing country inn. The innkeepers are two lively world travelers who speak French, Italian, German, and a little Arabic, and treat their guests like dear old friends. Sandra rides with the Rappahannock Hunt and encourages all visitors to enjoy a trailride through the Blue Ridge scenery.

The inn is furnished throughout with an eclectic blend of antiques and family treasures gathered from around the world. All are set off by the old stone fireplaces and low-beamed ceilings of the rooms. Sandra Cartwright-Brown is quick to weed out the faint of heart on the phone with accurate descriptions of the lack of certain modern amenities at the inn, such as central heating in several of the rooms. To stay here is to be whisked back to the eighteenth century, with its symphony of crackling fires, creaking stairs, century-old floors, and winds rattling across the old tin roof. One room with 18" thick walls has its own private entrance and porch. Breakfast is a gourmet affair; with advance notice, dinner is served to guests. The Conyers House is just minutes from a nouvelle French restaurant, the Inn at Little Washington. Sandra offers monthly seminars for prospective innkeepers.

Accommodations: 10 rooms, 5 with private bath. *Pets and children:* Not permitted. *Driving Instructions:* Write for detailed instructions. Sperryville is west of Washington, D.C., near Skyline Drive in the Blue Ridge Mountains.

Stanley, Virginia

JORDAN HOLLOW FARM INN

Route 626, Stanley, Virginia. Mailing address: Route 2, P.O. Box 375, Stanley, VA 22851. 703-778-2209 or 778-2285. *Innkeepers:* Marley and Jetze Beers. Open all year.

Jordan Hollow Farm offers guests a chance to enjoy country-inn comfort in the surroundings of a working two-hundred-year-old horse farm on rolling meadows at the foot of the Blue Ridge Mountains and Shenandoah National Park. The inn's oldest part, the restaurant, is housed within two log cabins built in 1790, with rooms added over the years. The "new" part of the house was completed in 1882, and an old lodge, horse barn, and hay barn are about the same age. Rowe's Lodge, designed to match the farmhouse in style, was built in 1984.

Innkeeper Jetze Beers is Dutch and moved to this country some years ago; he loves to entertain guests with anecdotes from his homeland. Marley is an artist and horsewoman, and she often can be found training the Holsteiner horses she raises for show jumping.

Public rooms at Jordan Hollow include a rustic bar and lounge where beer and wines are served and where there are occasional country-music evenings. The dining room offers all three meals to guests and the public. The dinner menu includes rib-eye steak, sautéed trout, quail, pork chops, ham, and broiled chicken breast.

Accommodations: 16 rooms with private bath. *Pets:* Not permitted, but a boarding kennel is nearby. *Driving Instructions:* From Luray, take Route 340 6 miles south, turn left on Route 624, left on Route 689, and right on Route 626.

Staunton, Virginia

FREDERICK HOUSE
  18 East Frederick Street, Staunton, Virginia. Mailing address: P.O. Box 1387, Staunton, VA 24401. 703-885-4220. *Innkeepers:* Joe and Evy Harman. Open all year.

Staunton is a historic Virginia town in central Shenandoah Valley, not far from Skyline Drive and the Blue Ridge Parkway. Its many early homes and businesses have benefited from the preservationist spirit pervading the area. Staunton is also the home of Mary Baldwin College and the Woodrow Wilson Birthplace.

Frederick House is actually three town houses built between 1810 and 1910, which have been restored and furnished with antiques, period pieces, and comfortable upholstered chairs and sofas. The brick buildings, which have classic lines and a balustered portico, have been painted a soft gray with white trim. Within, eleven rooms and suites have carpeted floors, colorful wallpapers, air-conditioning, and television. A Continental breakfast is served in guests' rooms or suites. Next door, an athletic club offers indoor swimming, and tennis is nearby. The Harmans, who are familiar with the area, can direct guests to the many local activities, including a walking tour of Staunton.

Accommodations: 11 rooms and suites with private bath. *Pets and smoking:* Not permitted. *Driving Instructions:* Take either I-81 or I-64 to Staunton. From I-81, take Route 250 west to Frederick House.

Trevilians, Virginia

Trevilians, a quiet area east of Charlottesville, is just remote enough to make enjoying the countryside the most important "activity" in these parts. Within driving distance is *Monticello*, the home of Thomas Jefferson and *Ash Lawn*, the home of James Monroe. Also nearby is Montpelier, the home of James and Dolly Madison and the birthplace of George Clark of the Lewis and Clark expeditions.

PROSPECT HILL

Route 613 near Zion Crossroads, Virginia. Mailing address: R.D. 1, Box 55, Trevilians, VA 23170. 703-967-0844. *Innkeepers*: Bill and Mireille Sheehan. Open all year except Christmas.

Prospect Hill lives up to what most people expect in a small, romantic Southern country inn. The original building dates from 1732, with additions as late as 1880. It is an intact example of a working Virginia plantation with its original outbuildings. Guest rooms have been created in the manor house and the slave quarters. Guests arriving for dinner are encouraged to stroll around the grounds or sit on the veranda getting acquainted. In the cooler weather, they frequently gather in the foyer and parlor and enjoy the fire in the fireplace. No menu is posted at the inn, and there is but one seating. After a blessing by innkeeper Bill Sheehan, a four-course dinner is served, with the selections changing daily (special diets accommodated with advance notice). Beer and wine are available with dinner, which is served Wednesday through Saturday only. Overnight guests are served a full breakfast in bed when they awaken (any time after 8 A.M.). Surrounded by 40 acres of property, the inn affords opportunities for hiking through woods and pastureland.

Rooms at the inn are furnished with some antiques and feature such touches as quilt-covered four-posters, and fireplaces in most of the rooms. The Sheehans go out of their way to make their guests feel at home. Although dinner is available to the general public, the real fun of a trip to the inn is staying in one of the attractive guest rooms.

Accommodations: 10 rooms with private bath. *Pets:* Not permitted. *Driving Instructions:* From Charlottesville, take Route 250 east 1 mile past Zion Crossroads. Take a left (north) on Route 613 and drive 3 miles to the inn. From Washington, D.C., go west on Route 66 to Warrenton, then take Route 29 south to Culpepper. Take Route 15 south to Gordonsville, then Route 33 east 8 miles to the stop sign. Turn left at the stop sign and go 100 feet, then turn right onto Route 613 and drive 7 miles to the inn.

Upperville, Virginia

GIBSON HALL INN

Route 50, Upperville, Virginia. Mailing address: Box 225, Upperville, VA 22176. 703-592-3514. *Innkeepers:* George and Karin Eldridge-Wilson. Open all year.

Upperville is a historic town in the heart of Virginia's hunt country, which has all manner of horse-related activities, such as stable tours, horse shows, and races. The area is surrounded by the Blue Ridge Mountains and is located just an hour from Washington, D.C.

Gibson Hall was built in 1832 by the Gibson family and owned by their descendants until 1983, when the estate was purchased and meticulously renovated as a bed-and-breakfast inn. The building retains its fine Federal- and Greek Revival-style architectural features. Oriental rugs are set on polished pine floors, the original chandeliers have been electrified, and marble fireplaces are a reminder of an elegant earlier era. In the evening, the Eldridge-Wilsons provide guests with an opportunity to get to know each other over complimentary Virginia wines and cheese, served by the fire in the formal dining room, where a country breakfast is also served. The guest rooms have either brass or four-poster beds; all but one have fireplaces. The honeymoon suite has a large brass bed, whirlpool bath, and skylight overlooking the Blue Ridge foothills.

Accommodations: 6 rooms, 4 with private bath. *Pets and small children:* Not permitted. *Driving Instructions:* The inn is on Route 50 West, 10 miles from Middleburg.

Vesuvius, Virginia

SUGAR TREE INN
Highway 56, Vesuvius, VA 24483. 703-377-2197. *Innkeepers:* The Schroeder family. Open mid-April through November.

Sugar Tree Lodge is a rustic country inn on the side of a mountain some 3000 feet up in Virginia's Blue Ridge Mountains. From the porch rockers, one can see 27 miles down the Shenandoah Valley or across to neighboring mountain meadows. The ride to the inn is an adventure in itself: a three-mile drive straight up the mountain, culminating in a hairpin turn down the gravel lane and across a log bridge spanning a rushing mountain stream. Here, tucked into the terraced mountainside, are the lodge and guest houses, each assembled in pioneer mountain traditions from several late eighteenth- and early-nineteenth-century Virginia log structures.

Inside the lodge are several antique-filled guest rooms, a dining room, a tavern, a solarium-greenhouse, and a terraced dining area facing right into the mountain, rising straight up. The rooms are furnished with Shenandoah antiques from the early nineteenth century, plus later oak and chestnut pieces. The lounge has comfortable soft leather couches grouped in front of a stone hearth and chimney, complete with a moosehead above the mantle.

Upstairs, the library has a log balcony overlooking the living room. Each guest room has its own fireplace and modern bath, along with antiques, quilts, and chinked log or barnsided walls.

The dining rooms are open to guests for breakfast and to the public for lunch and dinner. The blackboard menu offers French nouvelle cuisine using fresh local ingredients. The word is out and the restaurant is packed on weekends; reservations are a must.

Accommodations: 11 rooms, all with private bath. *Pets:* Not permitted. *Driving Instructions:* Take Route 11 about 17 miles north of Lexington to Steele's Tavern. Turn east on Route 56. The lodge is 2.8 miles past the village of Vesuvius.

MEADOW LANE LODGE

Route 39, Warm Springs, Virginia. Mailing address: Star Route A, Box 110, Warm Springs, VA 24484. 703-839-5959. *Innkeepers:* Philip and Catherine Hirsh. Open April through New Year's Day.

In the heart of the Virginia Allegheny Mountains lie Warm Springs and the Hirshes' 1,600 acres of woods, fields, and streams. The area is picture-postcard perfect in all seasons, and the Meadow Lane Lodge is a natural part of that scene, its pastoral setting, its lawn and bordering trim hedges, and its many varieties of wildflowers and birds providing an ideal home base for nature lovers of all kinds. Two miles of the Jackson River meander through the estate, and the Hirshes keep it well stocked with trout for fly-casting enthusiasts at the lodge. An Orvis Fly Fishing School is located at the lodge. Inquire for information.

Meadow Lane blends contemporary comfort and furnishings with antique pieces. The spacious living room has a pair of stone fireplaces with fires going on chilly mornings and evenings. A full country breakfast is served from a 1710 sideboard in the sunny porch-dining room. It is the only meal served, although the Hirshes will help guests with dinner reservations at any of the excellent restaurants in the area.

Meadow Lane Lodge accepts no more than twenty guests at a time, making the stay, for most, seem like a house party. The guest rooms vary from spacious doubles to suites with living rooms and fireplaces to a choice of private antique-filled cottages. Craig's Cottage is on the Meadow Lane estate and has its own fireplace. Francisco Cottage is on the steep hillside above Gristmill Square, in the village itself, with a full living room, brick fireplace, kitchen, a porch with a view of the surrounding hillside, and a comfortably furnished bedroom. The Car Barn, so named because the ground floor houses the Hirshes antique automobiles, has two guest rooms and a large living room.

Accommodations: 10 rooms with private bath. *Pets:* Inquire first. *Driving Instructions:* From Lexington on I-81, take Route 39 west to Warm Springs. From Roanoke, take Route 220. From Staunton, Virginia, on I-81, take Route 254 to Buffalo Gap, Route 42 to Millboro Springs, then Route 39 to Warm Springs. The lodge entrance is 4 miles west of Warm Springs on Route 39

Warm Springs is nestled in a beautiful valley in the Alleghenies; some of the valley rock formations are thought by geologists to be the oldest known. In Warm Springs Valley there is a rim of Ordovician older than the carbon beds where coal is found. The peaceful Victorian hamlet has churches and a cemetery dating from the 1800s, and the old ham house where Virginia hams once were processed. On Courthouse Square is an old law-office building that houses the Bath County Historical Society and its interesting collections of Indian artifacts and local families' heirlooms. It is open Friday and Saturday from 3 to 5, June through October. Gristmill Square is a restoration of old buildings that contains shops and a gallery showing local artists' works.

The actual Warm Springs bubbles up some 1,200 gallons of crystal-clear 96.5° water per minute. It has been a health spa since the Indian and colonial times.

Williamsburg, Virginia

WILLIAMSBURG INN AND COLONIAL HOUSES

South Francis Street, Williamsburg, Virginia. Mailing address: P.O. Drawer B, Williamsburg, VA 23185. 804-229-1000. *Innkeeper:* Russell E. Cleveland, Jr. Open all year.

The Williamsburg Inn, with its 235 rooms, is not strictly a country inn, but it is one of the country's finest and most attentive small hotels. It opened in 1937 as part of the Rockefeller plan for Williamsburg's development, and it bears his penchant for perfection. Largely furnished in the Regency manner, it has thick carpeting, formal settings,

274 / VIRGINIA

swagged draperies, and chandeliers. Distinguished visitors at the inn have included many presidents and other heads of state, as well as royalty. Some of the more formal meals in the Williamsburg Inn are served in the Regency dining room. Here the fading tradition of coats and ties for gentlemen is still upheld, though it has eased a bit for women, who are now admitted in pants suits. The inn offers the most elaborate overnight accommodations in the village, with many large suites available in both the original inn and its more recent guest wings, known as Providence Hall. A number of the suites in these modern buildings have fireplaces and private terraces overlooking the nearby golf courses and tennis courts.

The charm of a Williamsburg visit is enhanced by the many Colonial Houses that provide lodging within the historic village, with full hotel services provided by the Williamsburg Inn. Here, a country-inn atmosphere prevails. There are sixteen rooms in the dormered Brick House Tavern, and many rooms are tucked into converted colonial kitchens complete with the original fireplaces. Others still are in former shops that now provide overnight comfort for twentieth-century guests. At one time, the colonial laundry served the townhouse of an owner of a great plantation, who was a member of the Governor's Council. The laundry is now a one-room cottage in its own secluded garden. The Chiswell House is a white clapboard building reminiscent of a Virginia plantation home; the Market Square Tavern has survived from the early days of Williamsburg and now offers thirteen guest rooms and its restored living rooms. The furnishings of the Colonial Houses are in keeping with their period, with plenty of canopied beds as well as the modern convenience of air conditioning. These are by no means the only accommodations offered by Colonial Williamsburg. Others tend to be more motel-like but still maintain the high standard established by John D. Rockefeller, Jr., more than fifty years ago. There is a complete list of motels and guest houses in the area, and Colonial Williamsburg will be happy to steer you to alternatives.

Accommodations: 235 rooms with private bath, plus various accommodations in restored colonial houses. *Driving Instructions:* Take I-64 to Williamsburg. Follow the green information signs to the Colonial Williamsburg Information Center, where instructions to the inn or Colonial houses will be given.

Woodstock, Virginia

INN AT NARROW PASSAGE
U.S. 11 South at Route 672, Woodstock, Virginia. Mailing address: P.O. Box 83, Woodstock, VA 22664. 703-459-8000. *Innkeepers:* Ellen and Ed Markel, Jr. Open all year.

The Inn at Narrow Passage was built of squared logs in 1740 as part of a small Shenandoah frontier settlement. Strategically located at the "narrow passage" in the Shenandoah River Valley, it was the scene of many Indian attacks and a refuge for travelers on the turnpike. In 1803 it was enlarged to serve stagecoach travelers. During the Civil War, Stonewall Jackson headquartered here, his troops camping by the river and on the grounds surrounding the inn.

The Markels have restored and preserved the architectural integrity of this historic building. The rooms have exposed-log walls and beams, limestone fireplaces, and rag rugs on polished pine floors, along with Colonial antiques and period reproductions. Tin and pewter lighting fixtures are used throughout; walls are decorated with needlework and early prints. Fires crackle in the grates of the living room and guest rooms.

Ed and Ellen serve a Southern breakfast, which can be worked off right out behind the inn, where there is fishing, hiking, and rafting just steps away.

Accommodations: 6 rooms, 4 with private bath. *Pets:* Not permitted. *Driving Instructions:* Take exit 72 off I-81. The inn is on Route 11, 2 1/2 miles south of Woodstock.

Index of Inns

WITH ROOM-RATE AND CREDIT-CARD INFORMATION

Index of Inns

WITH ROOM-RATE AND CREDIT-CARD INFORMATION

Inns are listed in the chart that follows. In general, rates given are for two persons unless otherwise stated. Single travelers should inquire about special rates. The following abbreviations are used throughout the chart:

dbl. = double. These rates are for two persons in a room.

dbl. oc. = double occupancy. These rates depend on two persons being registered for the room. Rentals of the room by a single guest will usually involve a different rate basis.

EP = European Plan: no meals.

MAP = Modified American Plan: rates include dinner and breakfast. Readers should confirm if stated rates are per person or per couple.

AP = American Plan: rates include all meals. Readers should confirm if stated rates are per person or per couple.

BB = Bed and Breakfast: rates include full or Continental breakfast.

Credit-Card Abbreviations

AE = American Express MC = MasterCard
CB = Carte Blanche V = Visa
DC = Diners Club

Important: All rates are the most recent available but are subject to change. Check with the inn before making reservations.

Aerie, 153; rates: $75 dbl. BB; AE, MC, V
Anchuca, 115; rates: $75 to $105 dbl. BB; AE, MC, V
Annie's Bed & Breakfast, 203; rates: $48 to $115 dbl. BB; AE, MC, V
Ashby Inn, 261; rates: $60 to $90 dbl. BB; MC, V
Badu House, 219; rates: $45 to $60 dbl. BB; MC, V
Bailey House, 21; rates: $55 to $85 dbl. BB; AE
Ballastone Inn, 60; rates: $85 to $175 dbl. BB; AE, MC, V
Balsam Lodge, 123; rates: $28 to $40 dbl. BB
Baron's Creek Inn, 210; rates: $65 to $85 dbl. BB
Battery Carriage House, 174; rates: $88 dbl. BB; AE, MC, V
Bay Street Inn, 171; rates: $60 to $65 dbl. BB
Beaumont House, 25; rates: $38 dbl. BB
Beaumont Inn, 81; rates: $48 to $55 dbl. EP; MC, V
Bed and Breakfast Inn, 62; rates: $38 to $68 dbl. BB; AE, MC, V
Beverly Hills Inn, 37; rates: $62 dbl. BB; AE, MC, V
Boone Tavern Hotel, 77; rates on request
Buckhorn Inn, 185; rates: $60 to $80 dbl. BB
Burn, 105; rates: $60 to $125 dbl. BB; MC, V
Buttonwood, 145; rates: $35 to $55 dbl. BB

Casa de Solana, 28; rates: $75 to $125 dbl. BB; AE, MC, V
Castle Inn, 221; rates: $60 dbl. BB
Catlin-Abbott House, 262; rates: $73 dbl. BB; AE, MC, V
Cedar Grove Mansion, 117; rates: $75 and up dbl. BB; MC, V
Chalet Suzanne Inn and Restaurant, 26; rates: $75 to $125 dbl. EP, MAP available off-season
Channel Bass Inn, 237; rates: $100 to $175 dbl. EP; AE, DC, MC, V
Charm House, 42; rates on request
Clewiston Inn, 23; rates: $45 to $50 dbl. EP; AE, CB, DC, MC, V
Colonel Ludlow House, 169; rates: $55 to $98 dbl. BB; AE, MC, V
Commercial Hotel, 16; rates: $33 dbl. EP; AE
Conyers House, 264; rates: $80 to $100 dbl. BB
Cottage Plantation, 102; rates: $70 dbl. BB
Country Place Hotel, 207; rates: $27 to $37 dbl. EP
Crescent Cottage Inn, 7; rates: $55 to $65 dbl. BB; MC, V
Crystal River Inn, 227; rates: $45 to $60 dbl. BB; MC, V
Culpepper House, 72; rates: $45 to $50 dbl. BB
Dairy Hollow House, 8; rates: $69 dbl. BB, cottages $99 to $149; AE, MC, V
De Loffre House, 44; rates: $50 dbl. BB; AE, MC, V
Doe Run Inn, 79; rates: $20 to $35 dbl. EP; MC, V
Dogwood Inn, 136; rates: $45 dbl. BB
Donoho Hotel, 192; rates: $50 dbl. MAP
Duval House, 24; rates: $38 to $88 dbl. BB; AE, MC, V
Edwardian Inn, 12; rates: $44 to $47 dbl. BB; AE, MC, V
1842 Inn, 54; rates: $55 to $75 dbl. BB; AE, MC, V
Eliza Thompson House, 64; rates: $88 to $108 dbl. BB; AE, MC, V
Elliott House Inn, 175; rates on request
Eseeola Lodge, 150; rates on request
Esmeralda Inn, 137; rates: $27 to $75 dbl. BB; MC, V
Excelsior House, 214; rates: $30 to $55 dbl. EP
Farris 1912, 206; rates: $40 to $50 dbl. EP, hunting season $90 to $95 per person AP; AE, MC, V
Fish Pond Plantation, 245; rates: $65 dbl. BB
Fleur de Lis Inn, 89; rates: $55 dbl. BB; AE, MC, V
Flint Street Inn, 119; rates: $60 dbl. BB; AE, MC, V
Foley House Inn, 65; rates: $95 to $175 dbl. BB; AE, MC, V
Franklin Terrace, 146; rates: $40 to $44 dbl. BB; MC, V
Frederick House, 267; rates: $30 to $50 dbl. EP; AE, DC, MC, V
French Quarter Maisonnettes, 92; rates: $36 to $42 dbl. EP
Fryemont Inn, 128; rates: $80 dbl. MAP; MC, V
Gibson Hall Inn, 270; rates: $80 to $120 dbl. BB; AE, MC, V
Glencoe Plantation, 104; rates: $60 to $85 dbl. BB; MC, V
Graystone Guest House, 166; rates: $85 dbl. BB; AE, MC, V
Greyfield Inn, 45; rates: $85 to $90 per person AP; MC, V
Greystone Inn (Lake Toxaway), 149; rates: $85 to $160 per person MAP; AE, MC, V
Greystone Inn of Savannah, 65; rates: $70 dbl. BB

Hale Springs Inn, 194; rates: $35 to $65 dbl. BB; AE, MC, V
Hallcrest Inn, 164; rates: $60 dbl. MAP
Hamilton Garden Inn, 240; rates: $45 to $75 dbl. BB; DC, MC, V
Harmony House Inn, 154; rates: $65 dbl. BB; AE, MC, V
Hartwell Inn, 48; rates: $40 dbl. BB
High Cotton Inn, 200; rates: $50 to $65 dbl. BB
High Hampton Inn and Country Club, 133; rates: $118 dbl. AP; AE
Highland Inn (Monterey, VA), 257; rates: $39 to $49 dbl. EP; MC, V
Highlands Inn (Highlands, NC), 147; rates: $69 to $79 dbl. EP, suites available; AE, MC, V
Hillcrest Grove, 49; rates: $50 dbl. BB
Historic Country Inns (Lexington, VA), 250; rates: $65 to $80 dbl. BB; Choice, MC, V
Historic Rugby, Inc., 195; rates: $37 to $48 dbl. EP
Holland-Duncan House, 263; rates: $35 to $55 dbl. BB
Homestead The, 241; rates: $120 per person AP; AE, V
Homestead House Inn, 191; rates: $45 to $90 dbl. BB; AE, MC, V
Hotel Faust, 222; rates: $27 to $55 dbl. EP, suites $90; AE, CB, DC, MC, V
Hotel Jefferson, 215; rates: $45 to $75 dbl. EP
Hotel Maison de Ville, 94; rates: $110 to $350 dbl. BB; AE, CB, DC, MC, V
Indigo Inn, 177; rates: $85 to $95 dbl. BB; AE, MC, V
Inn, The, 173; rates: $35 to $65 dbl. BB
Inn at Bingham School, 135; rates: $75 to $85 dbl. BB
Inn at Levelfields, 241; rates: $55 to $65 dbl. BB; MC, V
Inn at Mountain View, 17; rates: $36 dbl. BB
Inn at Narrow Passage, 276; rates: $50 to $70 dbl. BB; MC, V
Inn on Providence, 152; rates: $50 to $65 dbl. BB; MC, V
Island Hotel, 22; rates: $50 to $65 dbl. BB
Jarrett House, 140; rates on request
Jordan Hollow Farm Inn, 266; rates: $65 dbl. EP; DC, MC, V
Kenwood Inn, 29; rates: $65 dbl. BB; MC, V
Kings Arms, 155; rates: $60 to $62 dbl. BB; AE, MC, V
La Borde House, 225; rates: $45 dbl. EP; AE, MC, V
La Colombe d'Or, 213; rates: from $150 dbl. BB; AE, DC, MC, V
Lafitte Guest House, 96; rates on request
Lake Rabun Hotel, 50; rates: $32 dbl. BB
Lamothe House, 97; rates: $65 to $95 dbl BB, suites to $150; AE, MC, V
Landmark Inn State Historic Site, 204; rates: $30 dbl. EP
LaPrade's Restaurant, Cabins, and Marina, 43; rates: $24 per person AP
Laurel Brigade Inn, 247; rates: $54 dbl. EP
Liberty Hall Inn, 184; rates: $65 dbl. BB; MC, V
Liberty Inn, 67 ; rates: $85 to $95 dbl. BB; AE, MC
Lickskillet Inn, 209; rates: $40 dbl. BB; AE, MC, V
Linden, 108; rates: $76 dbl. BB
Little River Inn, 234; rates: $65 to $185 dbl. BB; MC, V
Little Saint Simons Island, 52; rates: $250 dbl. AP; MC, V

Lords Proprietor's Inn, 142; rates on request.
Lowenstein-Long House, 190; rates: $50 dbl. BB, hostel rooms lower; MC, V
Magnolia Inn, 158; rates: $32 dbl. BB
Magnolia Place, 69; rates: $75 to $135 dbl. BB; AE, MC, V
Martha Washington Inn, 231; rates: $72 dbl. EP, suites higher; AE, DC, MC, V
Mayhurst, 260; rates: $72 to $85 dbl. BB
Meadow Lane Lodge, 272; rates: $79 to $105 dbl. BB; AE, MC, V
Megan Lorien House, 13; rates: $50 to $100 dbl. BB; MC, V
Meredith House, 220; rates: $55 dbl. BB; MC, V
Middleton, 188; rates: from $65 and up dbl. BB; MC, V
Milbank, 87; rates: $75 dbl. BB; MC, V
Mill Farm Inn, 162; rates: $48 to $60 dbl. BB
Mintmere Plantation House, 90; rates: $100 dbl. BB
Miss Molly's Inn, 238; rates: $59 to $88 dbl. BB
Monmouth Plantation, 109; rates: $75 to $100 dbl. BB; AE, MC, V
Morrison House, 235; rates: $115 to $330 dbl. EP; AE, DC, MC, V
Mount Holly House, 258; rates: from $55 to $65 dbl. BB
Murchison House, 168; rates: $60 dbl. BB; AE, MC, V
New Orleans Hotel, 11; rates: $75 to $95 dbl. EP
Norris House Inn, 248; rates: $55 to $90 dbl. BB
Nu Wray Inn, 130; rates: $45 dbl. EP
Nutt House, 212; rates: $35 to $60 dbl. EP; MC, V
Oak Square, 114; rates: $55 to $65 dbl. BB; AE, MC, V
Oakwood Inn, 159; rates: $60 to $70 dbl. BB; AE, MC, V
Old Edwards Inn, 148; rates: $75 dbl. BB; AE, DC, MC, V
Old Reynolds Mansion, 121; rates: $35 to $55 dbl. BB
Oliver-Britt House, 113; rates: $45 dbl. BB; AE, MC, V
Orchard Inn, 161; rates: $75 dbl. BB
Park Plaza, 35; rates: $60 to $110 dbl. BB; AE, DC, MC, V
Park View Guest House, 99; rates: $50 to $65 dbl. BB; MC, V
Pfeiffer House, 200; rates: $40 dbl. BB
Pine Crest Inn, 163; rates: $48 to $90 dbl. EP; MC, V
Pink Lady, 201; rates: $30 to $70 dbl. BB
Planters Inn, 177; rates: $85 to $160 dbl. EP; AE, DC, MC, V
Pride House, 217; rates: $45 to $75 dbl. BB; MC, V
Prince Solms Inn, 223; rates: $60 to $110 dbl. BB; MC, V
Prospect Hill, 268; rates: $90 to $120 dbl. BB, $140 to $170 dbl. MAP; MC, V
Ragged Garden Inn, 127; rates: $55 to $85 dbl. BB; AE, MC, V
Randolph House, 129; rates: $90 to $110 dbl. MAP; MC, V
Ray House Bed and Breakfast, 122; rates: $37 dbl. BB
Red Fox Inn and Tavern, 253; rates: $85 to $200 dbl. BB; AE, MC, V
Red Rocker Inn, 126; rates: $30 to $55 dbl. EP
Richard Johnston Inn, 239; rates: $50 to $100 dbl. BB; AE, MC, V
River Forest Manor, 124; rates: $45 to $75 dbl. EP; MC, V
Riverfront House, 252; rates: $38 to $60 dbl. BB

Sea View Inn, 183; rates on request
17 Hundred 90, 70; rates on request
1735 House, 21; rates on request
Shakertown at Pleasant Hill, 85; rates: $40 to $70 dbl. EP
Shellmont Bed & Breakfast Lodge, 39; rates: $70 dbl. BB; AE, MC, V
Silver Street Inn, 112; rates on request
Silver Thatch Inn, 236; rates: $75 to $95 dbl. BB; AE, DC, MC, V
Snowbird Mountain Lodge, 160; rates: $92 to $98 dbl. AP; AE, MC, V
Soniat House, 100; rates: $105 to $200 dbl. BB; AE, MC, V
Southard-House, 197; rates: $45 to $100 dbl. BB; AE, MC, V
Squire Watkins Inn, 141; rates: $44 to $60 dbl. BB, cottages $42 to $55 EP
Statesboro Inn, 73; rates: $40 to $95 dbl. BB; AE, MC, V
Stovall House, 59; rates: $65 dbl. BB
Sugar Tree Inn, Ltd., 271; rates: $80 dbl. BB
Susina Plantation Inn, 74; rates: $65 per person MAP
Swag, The, 164; rates on request
Sword Gate Inn, 179; rates on request
Tanglewood Manor House, 139; rates: $49 to $65 dbl. EP; AE, DC, MC, V
Tar Heel Inn at Oriental, 157; rates: $60 dbl. BB
Telfair Inn, 40; rates: $48 to $100 per person dbl. BB; AE, DC, MC, V
Three Chimneys of Knoxville, 189; rates: $45 to $55 dbl. BB
Trillium House, 259; rates: $80 to $90 dbl. BB, suites $120 to $140; MC, V
Two Meeting Street Inn, 180; rates: $55 to $110 dbl. BB
Vendue Inn, 181; rates on request
Victorian House Bed & Breakfast, 30; rates: $45 to $65 dbl. BB; MC, V
Victorian Inn, 211; rates: $85 to $125 dbl. BB; AE, CB, DC, MC, V
Victorian Inns of Marietta-Atlanta, 56; rates: $59 to $69 dbl. BB; MC, V
Vine Cottage Inn, 243; rates: $35 to $50 dbl. BB; MC, V
Von Minden Hotel, 228; rates: $15 to $30 dbl. EP; MC, V
Wakulla Springs Lodge, 33; rates: $40 to $60 dbl. EP; MC, V
Weimar Country Inn, 229; rates: $30 to $65 dbl. BB
Welbourne, 255; rates: $80 to $90 dbl. BB; AE
Westcott House, 32; rates: $75 to $125 dbl. BB; MC, V
Williams House, 14; rates: $48 to $68 dbl. BB
Williamsburg Inn and Colonial Houses, 274; rates: $135 to $175 dbl. EP; MC, V
Wise Manor, 218; rates: $49 dbl. BB
Woodfield Inn, 144; rates: $55 to $80 dbl. BB; AE, MC, V
Wonderland Hotel, 187; rates: $32 to $45 dbl. EP; MC, V
Worley Homestead, 47; rates: $50 to $70 dbl. BB; AE, MC, V
York House, 57; rates: $50 to $55 dbl. BB; MC, V

Send us your name and address...
...and we'll send you a free gift.

If you purchased this book, we'd like your name and address for our mailing list. Just supply the information below, and we'll send you your free gift.

I purchased this book at:

- ☐ Atticus
- ☐ Barnes & Noble
- ☐ B. Dalton Booksellers
- ☐ Bookland
- ☐ Books Inc.
- ☐ Crown Books
- ☐ Encore Books
- ☐ Hunter's Books
- ☐ J.K. Gill
- ☐ Kroch's & Brentano's
- ☐ Lauriats
- ☐ Marshall Field & Co.
- ☐ Paperback Booksmith
- ☐ Readmore
- ☐ Stacy's
- ☐ Taylors
- ☐ Upstart Crow & Co.
- ☐ Waldenbooks

Other:_____ (City)_____

I purchased this book on (approximate date):_____

Please send my free gift to:

Name:_____

Street or Box:_____

City_____ State_____ Zip_____

Please mail to:
The Compleat Traveler, c/o Burt Franklin & Co., Inc.
235 East 44th St., New York, N.Y. 10017 U.S.A.

THE COMPLEAT TRAVELER'S READER REPORT

To: *The Compleat Traveler*
    c/o Burt Franklin & Co., Inc.
    235 East 44th Street
    New York, New York 10017 U.S.A.

Dear Compleat Traveler:

I have used your book in _____ (country or region).
I would like to offer the following ☐ new recommendation, ☐ comment,
☐ suggestion, ☐ criticism, ☐ or complaint about:

Name of Country Inn or Hotel:

_____

Address: _____

_____

Comments:

Day of my visit: _____ Length of stay: _____

From (name): _____

Address _____

_____ Telephone: _____

THE COMPLEAT TRAVELER'S READER REPORT

To: *The Compleat Traveler*
    c/o Burt Franklin & Co., Inc.
    235 East 44th Street
    New York, New York 10017 U.S.A.

Dear Compleat Traveler:

I have used your book in _____ (country or region).
I would like to offer the following ☐ new recommendation, ☐ comment, ☐ suggestion, ☐ criticism, ☐ or complaint about:

Name of Country Inn or Hotel:

_____

Address: _____

_____

Comments:

Day of my visit: _____ Length of stay: _____

From (name): _____

Address _____

_____ Telephone: _____